WHAT PEOPLE ARE SAYING ABOUT WHEN 'WANT TO' BECOMES 'HAVE TO!'

"An absolute must-read for anyone who has the desire to make a difference in their life and, more importantly, the lives around them. Gary Highfield has lived every word of When 'Want To' Becomes 'Have-to!' *with contagious enthusiasm and passion. His stories will evoke emotions and dreams in its readers that may have been tucked away for some time. This is a book to read and re-read as you see your dreams become reality."* – Buck Orrison, Health Care Executive

"I first met Gary Highfield when he came to my outside office early one morning in the spring of 1987. He went to work for us the next week and has been a very good friend and one of the most outstanding salespersons I have ever known. He became our top salesperson the first month he was with us, and over the years never gave up that honor. Read Gary's book, follow his example, and you will be a better person for it – not only in sales and leadership but also in life." – Harry L. Hudson, Past Vice President, Cellular One

"Gary's message in When 'Want To' Becomes 'Have To!'*, drawn from a lifetime of rich, often challenging, and many times unusual experiences, is one he's uniquely equipped to tell. His story has been forged from hard work, determination, grit and God's grace. He gives new meaning to the phrase, 'never say die.' What he has to say – and the example he's become – are what many, many individuals need today."* – Robert J. Tamasy, journalist and author

WHEN 'WANT TO' BECOMES 'HAVE TO!'

Breaking the Chains That Are Holding You Back

GARY HIGHFIELD

This book is dedicated to the ones I love:

To Kimberly…CC

You are the love of my life. I would not be the man I am today without you. You are truly God's gift to me – I'm one lucky man. You have inspired me to greater heights with your kind spirit and loving heart. You're my best friend and confidante. Thanks for believing in me, and I look forward to spending the rest of our lives together.

To Neil

Neil, watching you grow up and become the man of your own family is something very special. You have a character that is rare among men; it's the ability to be strong and kind at the same time. You're a leader of men and your words have wisdom beyond your age. The rest of your life will be the best of your life. Keep reaching for the stars. I am honored to say I'm your Dad.

To Brian

Brian, your talents are endless and you've just begun to tap into the great future that lies ahead of you. Your ferocious courage is rare among men. I'm truly honored to be your Dad. You're the kind of dad I wish I had had growing up. You have a beautiful family and the sky's the limit for you. Thank you for the encouraging words that convinced me to write my book. I'm very proud of you.

To Camellia…Daddy's girl

Camellia, you're the icing on the cake of our family. I can't imagine what my life would have been like without you in it. Your smile has lifted me up when I was down, and your laughter is infectious. A room is changed the moment you walk in it. It's been a true pleasure watching you become the best wife and mother any man or child could dream of.
I love your go-for-it attitude.
I am and will always be your number one fan!

CONTENTS

FOREWORD

I have had the great privilege of calling Gary Highfield a friend and watching his actions for more than twenty-five years. I can tell you that every word you read in *When 'Want To' Becomes 'Have To!'* has been written to give an honest and very real account of a man who had ALL the cards in a deck stacked against him.

You will be hard-pressed to put these riveting and heart-wrenching stories down. Soon you will find yourself so encouraged and amazed that anyone who has endured what Gary has could live with such passion and love for all who come in contact with him. I assure you, you'll want what Gary has.

I met Gary when he had just begun his journey in sales and business. Gary had then, as he has today, such a positive outlook and engaging nature about him, no matter what the subject. He sold me my very first cell phone, back when a cell phone resembled a boat anchor. Gary was so enthusiastic, I couldn't refuse. The amazing part of it all was that he was very concerned with making sure I was happy with my decision. The thing that stands out to me, even today, is his desire to do what is right no matter the cost.

During the early years of our friendship, I didn't know anything about Gary's upbringing, or lack of it, but knew he had a great story to tell. Over the years he would reveal more and more to me. He would follow it up by saying, "I feel God has called me to make a difference in lives of people" – and that is exactly what he has his sights on. You will begin to feel as if you've become friends with Gary as you read the words that are truly part of his very soul, poured out on the pages.

Gary has reached a place of success that many only hope for. He will be the first one to tell you that through a fervent faith, prayer and love for people, your life too can and will make a difference to all those around you. Gary and that little blonde-haired girl who locked her keys in the car, Kimberly, have raised three great children who are successful in their chosen fields, and they also are blessed with eight beautiful grandchildren.

Through resolve and hard work, Gary has achieved more than just monetary success. He has, by God's grace, altered the very roots of his family tree that will leave a lasting heritage for generations.

Everyone that picks up this book can be assured of experiencing and learning from the life of someone with a real passion to encourage you on your own personal journey.

When 'Want To' Becomes 'Have To!' is an absolute must-read for anyone that has the desire to make a difference in their life and, more importantly, the lives around them. Gary has lived every word of this book because deep inside he "Had To," and has done so with contagious enthusiasm and passion. The stories drawn from his life will evoke emotions and dreams in you the reader that may have been tucked away for some time. This is a book to read and re-read as you strive to see your dreams become reality.

– *Buck Orrison, Health Care Executive*

'WANT TO'
By Gary Highfield

What would you do to succeed?
How many times would you try?
How many things would you try?
How many people would you talk to?
How many books and CDs would you be willing to read and listen to?

This thing called success.
Your friends might say, "Don't give up your good job down at the factory
They'll take good care of you."
*They might say, "Sales? You **WANT TO** get into sales? Ha, ha!*
There is nothing sure about sales."
For you have only yourself to count on in sales.

I challenge you to start stretching yourself today, taking small steps at first.
I challenge you to let go of your past feelings of doubt. And start to see yourself in a
different light, the light of your dreams.
I challenge you to reveal your dreams; but be prepared; because those closest to you may
be the very ones who will discourage you the most.
For you and only you can allow the light of your dreams to go out.

What would you do to succeed?
You must be willing to open yourself up: And step into the glare of criticism.
And you must be willing to go it alone if necessary, with only hope and faith to carry
you through.

How many opportunities could you look back on in your life?
Whether it was a ball game or a contest or maybe another job?
When you just let it slip through – you could have done it but you just let it pass:
How many times?
Commit yourself to the dreams, refusing to look back and never letting go.
For it's much easier to explain how you did it…than why you didn't.
Get yourself a David and Goliath-sized dream – and go for it.

All it takes is WANT TO!

INTRODUCTION

What are you willing to do about your own circumstances?

This book is about breaking chains – the chains that were holding me back from using the talents I'd been given. These chains holding me back were fear of the unknown; no experience; limited education, and no people skills. To go along with these chains, I had other disadvantages: I didn't know how to dress for success. And I'd never even heard the word, résumé. These were my chains, but the time came when I refused to use them as excuses.

You may have some chains holding you back, too.

I don't know where you are in the big game of life. You may be starting on the one-foot line with your back to the goal line. Or you may be farther along in life, closer to the fifty-yard line. Maybe you're about to score your first big win. It doesn't matter where you're starting out; what matters the most is you are giving this game of life your best shot. My goal is for you to finish this book and when you're done I want you to say, "Put me in, coach!"

The goal line is the same for everyone. "Nobody can go back and start a new beginning, but anyone can start today and make a new ending," Maria Robinson wisely said. Some will say to you, "There's no use trying. You'll never get out of this place." But don't believe that for a minute. Jim Rohn says, "Give up the blame game – what happens, happens to all of us."

I'm about to ask you to take some very bold actions, mountain-moving actions. I'll be asking you to change for one main reason: If you will, everything around you will change. Your day is today. When your life flashes before your eyes – and it surely will – make it worth watching.

My hope in writing this book is to give encouragement to people like me who were not born with the proverbial silver spoon in their mouths or raised in the best of circumstances. I'm writing especially to those who feel they are powerless to change their situation and improve their lives. My goal is to provide some insight into a childhood and early adult life that may have been just as desperate and difficult as the lives many others remember – or possibly the way it is today for you, or for someone you know.

Each of us is born into a different situation – good, bad or ugly. However, no matter what your situation is, no matter how desperate or hopeless it may seem, you do have the ability to become all you *want to* be...that is, if you *want to* badly enough. I believe that statement with all my heart. If you are living in a volatile environment, I *want to* help you strive with everything you have inside you to find the courage, the initiative and the will power to do whatever you need to do to get out of the hole you find yourself in.

I'm sharing my story with you so you can understand and evaluate the effort I made. I want you to see the changes I undertook in my own life that propelled me forward, toward a new career, a new outlook on life, and a *brighter future* for my family. I have worked hard all my life and it required a tremendous amount of effort and many changes to get where I am today, enjoying a successful career in the financial world and reaching out to others with a positive message about life. And I'm not finished yet.

My intent for this book is simple. I want you to know that you have what it takes to change the life that's ahead of you. It will take some time, and lots of effort, but I promise – it's worth it. I can testify to this. In fact, the more effort you give, the further you'll move the mark. You can achieve goals and reach heights you never dreamed possible, but you have to try.

You need to understand and believe a simple fact: We're all created with God-given abilities. However, deep-seated feelings of doubt, fear and insecurity can immobilize you, stopping you in your tracks before you can start exploring the uncertain but exciting future. I compare our God-given abilities to yeast in a loaf of bread. It's there, but it needs the opportunity to rise. Perhaps you've suppressed this "yeast," afraid of the unknown, but these talents and gifts from God are what make you special and unique. If you want to change what you *do,* then it's going to require you to change what you *believe.*

Have you ever flown in an airplane – or even seen a plane take off in a movie? You rise into the clouds, and for a few moments you can't see a thing. Then suddenly you rise above the clouds and everything becomes crystal clear. That's what it's like when you finally decide to put your ***want to*** into action. At first it's cloudy, but then you start to see the life you can have for your family. *That new life can start today!*

One of the main messages I hope and pray you will take away from reading this book is the power of setting goals and then pursuing them with all your might. Goals, I've found, have the power of lightning. When you set them and embark on a plan for achieving them, an immeasurable power is unleashed. Your mind will start to formulate a plan to achieve them. And it starts with a simple act of writing them down. After you have written them down, you instantly have a target to aim for, a direction to follow. In the corporate world they call this kind of single-mindedness a "mission statement" – and you're about to start a mission.

Then you take a second, equally simple but very important step: *Action.* You begin to do something about those goals. Putting goals into words is a great first step, but they have no value until you're determined to do something about them. Nothing happens until you take action. Believe me, your dreams are screaming out your name!

That's why I'm offering my story to you. It's not about me. I don't want to impress you with my story. I want you to see how I went about changing the lifestyle I could offer my family, which included raising my yearly income level almost seven times. The specific steps you decide to make will probably be different from mine. I'm sure they will be, because we're all different and the road we must travel is unique. But the basic steps for getting out from "under the circumstances" and realizing your dreams are the same.

For me, it all started when I came to the undeniable conclusion that I needed to make some personal changes. This was when my ***want to,*** my dreams for having a better life, turned into ***have to!*** I couldn't wait any longer. And I hope you won't wait any longer than the time it takes to read this book – and maybe you'll get started before that.

My *want to* turned into *have to* when I realized nothing I was doing seemed to be making any difference. Nothing was changing; I was spinning my tires in the same rut, day after day. What I hadn't realized up to that point was I wasn't ready for a new career and a new life. Before I could start climbing out of the hole I was in, months before I could start to use my talents, I had some work to do. I needed a lot of polishing – and more polishing and more polishing.

There were days, I'll admit, when I considered giving up. The days went on and on with no sign of assurance that anything was ever going to change. But I'll promise you, they will change, and they will change for you. Quitting can never be an option for you or me. And looking back, I can state without any hesitation that it's been worth it. Every minute, every ounce of effort was worth it.

When I reflect back on the days that led up to our new life, the steps that it took to get there, I can clearly see how everything came together. When I was ready, my new life was waiting for me and the doors began to open up. The talents that lay dormant within me for so many years, like yeast that hasn't permeated the dough, were there waiting to rise. You know the adage about "the best thing since sliced bread"? *You can be better – much better – than sliced bread!*

What happened in my life can happen for you. The talents you have may not be the same as those of someone else, but God has given them to you for a reason. And if you put them to work, willing to test them to the maximum, you will be rewarded. I can assure you of that.

Throughout this book I've included some quotations that have proved helpful to me. Many are from books I've read or people I've heard speak. The ones marked G.H. are my own, thoughts and insights that have come to me through the years. I've also incorporated two sets of lists: *Some Thoughts for You to Consider,* and *Action Steps.* This book isn't just about talking about making change – it's about doing something about it.

One last word before we start to work. By the way, don't you like that word, *"work"?* It's a good word – and to get from where you are now to where you want to be will require work. But you're not going to believe what's about to happen. *It's been arranged for you to have someone with you every step of the way. You'll figure out who it is as we go along on this journey.*

My warning is simple: You will probably find people coming out of the woodwork with one thing in mind – to discourage you. "Who do you think you are, trying to be somebody?" "You don't have any experience!" "You can't do that!" I've heard these things and more. But just because people say it, that doesn't mean it's true. The truth is, they're wrong. You *can* do it, and I'm about to tell you how.

If you will refuse to give up, everything *will* change. It took me 1,740 days to get ready for my new life. I don't begrudge a single one of those days; they were all steps taking me – and my family – to where we are today. So don't get discouraged when the changes you want to see don't transpire in a few days, weeks or even months. Remember: True, lasting change takes time. It's going to require you to rethink the way you feel and react to the world around you.

If you will work hard, you will begin to see separation from the things that have been holding you back. The more preparation you do, the more separation you will get. The question is, how far do you want to go? As the old saying goes, "If I can do it, anyone can." Take charge of your life. Be willing to make the necessary changes and you will grow and realize your dreams. When you do, you'll find that you can see *RED: You can...Realize Every Dream.*

'THE BENCHMARK'

What is a benchmark? Why would I be talking about a benchmark? How can parents set benchmarks for their children to adhere to? The definition of benchmark is "a standard or point of reference against which things may be compared, assessed or measured."

This idea of a benchmark has become important to me for several reasons. The first one is the driving force inside me to set an example of what's possible if only you will try.

My gift for a wife, Kimberly, has set benchmarks for our daughter, Camellia. First of all, Camellia knows without any hesitation that she's loved by her Mom and Dad. Camellia has been given a road map to follow to help her in raising her own children. And nothing has been left to chance. From the diapers to the baths to the storybook reading, it's all there for her to recall at any time. The benchmarks Kimberly set give Camellia a starting point. There's no doubt Camellia has her own ideas about how she wants to raise her children. But the benchmarks are there for her to use as guides, and I'm certain she'll be setting new benchmarks for her own children to follow.

I'm convinced the chains holding us back in life can be broken and shaken off. As you read the chapters in my book, I hope you can pull from the words the benchmarks that have been laid down.

I believe we are all setting benchmarks every day of our lives. Everything you do is being observed by your children and everyone else around you. Your actions are captured in the mind's eye of everyone.

Yes, you are a benchmark. No matter what you believe, it's true. The question is what kind of benchmark are you? Are you a good, reliable benchmark for what to do or what not to do? Decide today to be the benchmark God intended you to be.

CHAPTER ONE

SOME THOUGHTS FOR YOU TO CONSIDER

*"In order to make anything a reality,
you have to dream about it first."*
Adora Svitak

"Belief is the rocket fuel for your dreams."
G.H.

- *Are you wondering what's out there for you?*

- *You can win with a losing hand.*

- *The jawbone talks about it, the wishbone dreams about it, and the backbone runs toward it and stands his ground.*

- *The person you respect is the person you should be asking how they achieved success. Talking to "Mr. Po Mouth" and listening to him verbalize negative thinking will not help you.*

- *The only time you'll ever pick up speed is when you're coasting downhill.*

- *What does it take to set a man free? Courage and a dream. What does it take to set a man free? A backbone of steel and a heart of gold. What does it take to set a man free? Being willing to listen carefully — and act on what you hear.*

- *If you have the ability to make a difference, then it's your responsibility to do so.*

- *If you have the ability to do something and you don't do it, shame on you.*

- *How do you move a mountain? One shovel at a time and hold it close to the blade.*

- *What would happen if you took everything you have learned, put it on the tip of a spear, and aimed it at the rest of your life?*

- *If you fail to plan, you're planning to fail.*

- *What would you do with the rest of your days if you were told today you have an incurable, terminal disease?*

- *Life's too short not to experience it.*

- *Everyone you meet is important — and the interest you show them, or don't show them, will come back to you in one way or another.*

- *Be careful not to separate your children too far from the work. If you do, you'll pay for it when they grow up.*

CHAPTER ONE

BORN A NOBODY, WANTING TO BE SOMEBODY

"Don't end up messed up."
G.H.

In our society today it's easy to feel like a victim. In fact, sometimes it's encouraged: Born to disadvantaged circumstances, raised in a difficult environment, surrounded by turmoil, and damaged by a broken home. The list of reasons could go on and on, but I'm convinced they're excuses that we use to justify not trying. Having been a product of disadvantaged circumstances, a difficult environment to grow up in, a broken home often in turmoil, I understand. But for whatever reason, I was determined not to use the excuses. I wanted my family to have a life, and the four jobs I had weren't providing it. That changed when my *want to* finally turned into *have to,* my life began to change.

But before I tell you how that came about, you need to know some things about me. The Gary Highfield that could have taken a wrong turn, a fatal wrong turn in life, but by the grace of God, I escaped. This is my story.

I was born to a single parent. My mom's name was Sara and she was almost nineteen years old when I came into the world. She was the youngest of six children, with three brothers and two sisters. Mom was a cheerleader when she was in the ninth grade. I still have her "CV" letters, the kind that were sewn on the front of a high school sweater back in those days. Mom often talked about how she wished that she had stayed in school. So when the time came, it was a big deal for her to see me finish high school and go to college.

Mom worked hard all her life to provide for my half-brother and me. She did the best she could. It was obvious, even then, that she had a lot of *"want to"* in her, and I know I inherited my get-up-and-go trait from her. She was one of those people who are generous to a fault, willing to give you the shirt off her back if necessary, but just as willing to punch you in the nose if you needed it. Mom could give you a look — one that would make your skin crawl if she was upset with something. She didn't like "high falootin'" people or the "fur-collar crowd" as she called them. She believed and, often enough, said most people have "a steak appetite and a baloney billfold."

After Mom quit high school in the ninth grade she worked at the Miller's department store in downtown Chattanooga. That was where she met my dad, my biological father. She also worked in the restaurant business, and the year after I graduated from high school we worked together at a private restaurant club on Lookout Mountain. She worked for the Tennessee Valley Authority (TVA) for several years, but was laid off.

Mom was quite a resourceful woman. She had to be. She started her own cleaning business and ran it for twenty years, with as many as five employees. Mom's policy was simple and direct: The floors should be so clean enough to eat off of them. Pride, detail, and *"want to"* were her gifts to me. When Mom cleaned something it would look brand new when she was finished. She had an extreme eye for detail. She used to tell me about scrubbing the floors in our apartment on her hands and knees. She didn't want me crawling around on a dirty floor. Mom didn't mind getting her hands dirty.

Mom had an extra bedroom in our small house and turned it into an "efficiency," as she called it. The rent from the apartment was another source of much-needed income. When I didn't have a car, Mom would walk to work so I could drive her car to school. I knew how much she loved me. Mom paid her own way and was never broke — only broken-hearted.

It's a shame sometimes things just don't seem to work out for some people. When you continue to make bad decisions, back-to-back, a situation can go from bad to worse. For most of my life, I watched this happen to my mom. In her eyes, I could always see the heartache from the love she failed to find. Through it all, though, she never lost her get-up-and-go. Never. She was quick with a smile, but the sorrow always showed through. The smile was simply her way of hiding the pain she felt inside. I will never know why she couldn't succeed in finding a lasting relationship. Mom always said she was looking for my father's replacement.

My father only came to see me once, when I was about a year old. My aunt told me he came to my grandmother's house where Mom and I lived and asked if he could see me. My aunt said when he came into the house, he sat down on the couch and she handed me to him. He placed me on his knee, and I suppose he just sat there looking at me. Later, he sat me on the floor. My aunt gave me one more image for my mind's eye: She said I kept untying my dad's shoelaces.

Maybe seeing me was all that my father needed at the time. He only stayed a few minutes. He left and I never saw him again. Good Lord, why did he do what he did? I have to wonder if he decided at that moment he was never going to see me again. Did the days turn in weeks, the weeks into months, and the months into years? What would make a father leave his own son and never *want to* see him again? Did he think I wasn't his child?

From time to time I still go back and drive by the old neighborhoods and look at the old houses we lived in. I can't comprehend how a dad could decide to see his son just once in a lifetime and be content with never seeing him again. How, in the love of God, can someone do that to a helpless child?

He must have carried with him an agonizing amount of pain and anguish for the rest of his short life. Something he felt inside was more than he could overcome that day – and for the rest of his days. Maybe in the next life he'll tell me what happened; they'll be no hurt feelings there. My dad leaving me has heightened my senses to the pain we can dish out so freely.

The absence of words between my father and me left a deep scar on my heart, but time marches on and dilutes the pain. I'm good now: My wife, Kimberly, and I have had a blessed life through seeing our three children grow up, and now we are watching our eight grandchildren grow up as well.

My father was an only child who was pampered and spoiled by his mother. As a little boy he was not allowed to play with his cousins or any other family members. Why was this? Because, I was told, they just were not good enough for him. He was a star athlete and played basketball at Sale Creek High School, just north of Chattanooga. He was six feet, four inches tall, and Mom was five-feet-two.

A few years ago, I was at Sale Creek High School for a basketball game with one of our grandkids. I walked around the halls of the old section of the school to see if I could find some of the trophies from years ago with dates matching when he would have played there. It was surreal to be walking the same halls he had walked. That day, so many years later, thoughts of him were still with me. I wondered if he ever stood exactly where I was standing and looked at the same trophy cases I was looking at.

My father, James E. Aslinger, was the tallest player on his basketball team at Sale Creek High School. I first saw this photo after Mom had passed away. It was hidden in an old trunk she kept in her bedroom.

Before Mom passed away I had only seen a couple of old photographs of my father. She had never shown me any of the pictures she had of him. Later, we found all the old photos she had. There he was posing with the other members of those basketball teams from years ago. In a strange way, I was proud of his accomplishments as an athlete, but I'll never understand why Mom hid picture after picture of him from me.

She even had one photo of him in the cap and gown he wore graduating from high school.

I have wondered to this day why things turned out the way they did. Sometimes it seems that for most of my life I've been working on a mystery without any clues. I can only imagine how their lives could have been. The unrealized possibilities the two of them would have had if only they had stayed together. They both had the inner drive, the looks, and plenty of *want to.* Enough to accomplish anything they set their minds to do. In my view, they both wasted their opportunity to be a family and spend their lives together. One fact I do know: They quit before they got started.

After my father graduated from high school, he went to work for a prominent building supply chain in downtown Chattanooga. He got himself into a lot of trouble for selling lumber to builders on the side. I never learned all the facts about the situation, just fragments of the story. When he was caught, my grandparents sold everything they had to keep him out of prison. They managed to keep him from being incarcerated, but staying in Chattanooga and facing everyone was too unpleasant. So they left Chattanooga and moved to St. Petersburg, Florida, and started a citrus farm.

The day they left Chattanooga they came to see me. I can still remember seeing my grandfather and grandmother in a flatbed truck, pulling away from my maternal grandmother Carlton's house where we lived. My grandfather on my dad's side leaned out the truck window, looked back at me, and waved goodbye as they drove away. That vision of my grandfather still lingers in my head.

I saw my grandfather one more time before he passed away, when Mom and I spent some time in Florida on their citrus farm. I rode through the orange groves with him on his green John Deere tractor and watched the farm hands plant orange trees. There's no telling what I could have grown up to be if I had been able to spend more time with my grandfather Aslinger. He was a good businessman who knew how to get things done. No one has ever told me what happened to the farm in Florida. I've been a salesman for many years, so who knows – I might have been selling orange juice today. I know the entrepreneur spirit I have inside comes from my grandfather, J.E. Aslinger.

My father left Chattanooga for Detroit, Michigan, where he worked for the Cadillac division of General Motors for thirty years. I don't remember when I learned that he worked for General Motors, but I'm proud of that fact. I suppose it was something to hold onto, something positive. Why would my dad have come to see me only one time, left town, and never come back? How could he live with himself? I truly can't imagine doing such a thing to a child. The grief he must have felt at times as the days he worked at GM slowly slipped away. I say that because I came from him. When one of my children calls or speaks to me, it lifts me up and makes my day. My dad chose to miss out on his son's life. Even today, I can't comprehend a decision of that magnitude.

Later I was told he had seven children with another woman he never married. I'll probably never know whether this is true or not. It really doesn't matter anyway. I have everything that's important: a great wife, family, and friends that I love.

I've only talked to my dad once in this lifetime. After I was grown and married, he called to say he was planning to come to Chattanooga to see Mom and me. Apparently, he was making some kind of effort to rekindle his relationship with Mom. But it never happened. I never heard from him again after that one and only phone call.

About ten years later, I got a phone call from a cousin on my father's side of the family, letting me know my dad had passed away. He had been dead for two weeks when I got the call. Who knows why they waited so long to tell me? Or why they even bothered to tell me at all? My father was fifty-seven years old when he died; I was told he had cirrhosis of the liver. But I will always believe he grieved himself to death over what he did to Mom and me. I guess it's important for me to believe he cared about us. I'll never stop wondering whether he thought about me as he was leaving this world. But I'm living my life now, and I've concluded – it really doesn't matter who your daddy was.

There's a verse in Paul Simon's song, "Slip Sliding Away," that seems fitting. It goes, *"And I know a father who had a son. He longed to tell him all the reasons for the things he'd done. He came a long way just to explain. He kissed his boy as he lay sleeping. Then he turned around and headed home again."* That's what my dad did: He slipped, and then he slid away, never to be seen again. It doesn't have to be this way for you – you can change it.

Until recently, I have never felt or experienced what it's like to have a dad. Then I found Psalm 66:5 in the Bible. In it I discovered that I did have a father after all. It reads, "A father to the fatherless, a defender of widows, is God in his holy dwelling." I'm sorry that it took me so long to learn this. When I read this verse for the first time, I realized my Heavenly Father had been there for me all along. I had lived with a feeling of emptiness my entire life, and for the first time I had someone to talk to about anything and everything – and I've learned this Father has all the right answers. There's something else, too. There is nothing He cannot do, and He wants me to be the best I can be. And over time I've learned that He gives me what I need – even if it's not always what I want.

He's never too busy, day or night, and He's always home. It was a very emotional moment to realize that I had such a Father and a friend all along. He was watching over me when I was walking down the road to the gas station where Mom's boyfriend worked when I was six years old. He was with me when I wasn't going to school in the third grade, when I would skip school and walk back home instead. He has given me courage to fight a good fight. All this time He was holding my hand, guiding me through His Holy Spirit.

CHAPTER ONE
ACTION STEPS

- Find the good in your parents. There are some things they did or didn't do that you can use in your life. It will help you with your family. Write these things down and consider your life with or without their influence.

- When you write the positive things down, it will help you to forget the negative thoughts and focus on the positive.

- Write down everything you can think of that made you happy and made you feel loved.

- Write down everything you can remember that was bad or difficult in your relationship with your parents. Then forgive them – and burn the paper you used to write down the bad things.

- Remember: The past is gone, and your future is waiting. Concentrate on that.

- Dwelling on all your unanswered questions from the past means living in the past and failing to consider the future. Your future can be anything you want it to be.

- No one has lived a mistake-free life. Some people have simply failed to learn from their mistakes. You're not one of those people, or you would not be reading this book. You are going to accomplish something good.

- Make a list of anyone toward whom you have ill feelings or against whom you are holding a deep grudge. Go to them and say you're sorry. It makes no difference how they respond. The release of tension, laying down a heavy burden, is liberating. You will be free at last from the past. Now you can get on with your life.

CHAPTER TWO

SOME THOUGHTS FOR YOU TO CONSIDER

"To climb steep hills requires slow pace at first."
William Shakespeare

- *A good sales representative is like water. You must find a way over, around, under, or through to whatever it is you are after.*

- *Have you ever experienced a day when you worked as if it was your last day on Earth? Is there anything you would die for?*

- *If you stay ready, you don't have to **get** ready.*

- *Golf headline: "John Survives at Pebble Beach." He "survives" at Pebble Beach? Give me a break.*

- *Consider not filling ourselves up with the things of this world, so we can have room to receive what God has to offer us: His blessings.*

- *There's only so much time in this life: There are approximately 43,800 minutes in every month. When you're young, time passes like an hour hand. When you're a little older, it moves with the pace of the minute hand. But when you finally get it together, time moves as quickly as the second hand. Don't you think it's time you get moving?*

CHAPTER TWO

'ONLY' EIGHT ELEMENTARY SCHOOLS

"Sometimes life changes whether you want it to or not."
G.H.

People say that children are resilient, that they're able to adjust to change. I agree with that. But when your life consists of constant change, there's only so much even an adaptable child can endure. In my early childhood life if I didn't like what was going on, I only had to wait a few days or weeks. And without fail, things would change – often dramatically.

For you to understand where I came from, the twisting and turning path my life took throughout my childhood, I have to tell you about some of those changes. Some were good, many were bad. But they all played a part in shaping the person I would become. As you'll see, the question was not whether I would like the changes but rather, how I would respond to them.

Do you know what life looks like when it's coming apart at the seams? Well I'm about to show you – from my own life experiences. I wasn't old enough to understand some things, the complicated things that adults face, but Mom was about to bring about some big changes in my life. I'm not saying I was hurt by what we were doing – as a child I didn't understand why we had to move around the country – but at the same time it was hard to feel at ease with the ever-changing circumstances in which we lived.

In the short span of only eighteen months, from the middle of the second grade to the beginning of the fourth grade, I went to eight different elementary schools, and lived in five different states, as my mother followed different men she had become involved with to different parts of the country. I was beginning to fall behind in my education with the constant moving from school to school. Some of the teachers quickly became frustrated with me. There were so many things that I should have known, so much I should have learned, but with the continual moving I had missed a lot of class time.

Today when I look back I realize there were times when we were living in nice, new homes (at least from my perspective), but my mom still wasn't happy. I'll never know the answer to why she was so unhappy. By that point, Mom had already been married four times. Her life was upside-down, but she had no clue for how to get it turned right-side up.

For a little boy without any roots, even seemingly minor things were important to me. For instance, one day my teacher took my yo-yo away from me; it was one of those really good ones, a beautiful pearl color. I don't remember what I did to make her take it away, but I'm sure I must have done something. I really didn't have any friends, and playing with the yo-yo was something I enjoyed. When she took it away, I was upset. It was one of the few things I really owned. But I did get the yo-yo back. A few days later, I asked the teacher for it, and she was nice to give it to me. It seems like a small thing, but I remember at the time it meant a lot to me.

In the mornings when I was in the third grade, it wasn't unusual for me to start out for school and then change plans. One of the schools I attended, Woodmore Elementary, was only a few blocks away. But when I would get to the school I often would walk right on by and go around the block and back home. I would hide behind our house so the neighbors couldn't see me and wait for the other kids in the neighborhood to come home from school. As far as I know, Mom never knew I skipped school many times in the third grade.

During this time I was one troubled little boy. The Big Brother I had been assigned from the Big Brother Association had quit picking me up. Mom had boyfriends in and out of our house. And I was getting into fights with boys after school as we were walking home. There wasn't anything good going on in my life at this time that I can remember. Is it any wonder my yo-yo was such a treasure to me?

Since we moved around frequently, I repeated the third grade for two years. This is one of those things that kids try to hide, but often other kids would figure it out anyway. Good memories from this time in my life are virtually nonexistent.

Our first real home was a house in Tiftonia, a small community near Chattanooga, Tennessee. I can remember riding my bicycle up and down the road in front of our house while leaning over the front handlebars, sticking my chest out like Mighty Mouse did on TV, and watching my grandpa, Mom's dad, sowing grass seed. Before this, we had only lived at my grandmother's house in the suburb of St. Elmo and then on Tennessee Avenue, not far from my grandmother's place for a short time. Today, when I go bicycle riding with the Chattanooga Bike Club, I see all the places where we lived. Sometimes it's difficult to believe how many moves we made. After four more moves, we finally settled into a permanent trailer home in the East Brainerd area.

Along the way, we made several moves away from Tennessee. For about a year, we lived in Fort Worth, Texas. I don't remember a lot about Texas except going to an Air Force base where my stepfather, T. Highfield, was stationed. He was one of four stepfathers I had, if you count him twice. Even though my biological father was an Aslinger, I got my last name from this stepfather.

We moved to Long Beach, California, for a short time, when Mom got a divorce and remarried again. My fondest memory of Long Beach was seeing a kid riding a skateboard down the sidewalk. It was the coolest thing I'd ever seen. We also lived in Cincinnati, Ohio for six or seven months. While we were there, getting to school in the mornings was a scary venture. I would walk to the bus stop before daylight to catch a city bus. No one walked me to the bus stop. This didn't add up; I couldn't understand how it was supposed to work. How would the bus driver know where I was going? How would I know where to get off and where get back on? It overwhelmed me, but somehow as a kid you just make it through these situations.

This portrait of my mom, Sara, predated the painful struggles she experienced later in life. Her sweet, peaceful pose reflected none of the drive and determination she mustered to endure incredible hardship.

Mom thought Cincinnati was the coldest place on earth. We never saw the grass, with snow covering the ground the entire time we lived there. From Cincinnati, we soon headed south to Tennessee again where our family lived.

We didn't stay anywhere for very long. It was six months here, six months there, and then we would pack up and leave again. Why did we stay on the move? Maybe Mom was looking for something positive, something stable, something she could build a life around. She never stopped looking. During this period of my life, about ten years, we moved fifteen times. I can still remember the last days at some of the places where we lived. I was always building some kind of tree house or hideout in the woods, and then Mom would yell for me to come in the house and away we would go to a new place.

As for my stepfathers, T. Highfield and my mother were married twice. Things never did work out for them. Then there was Clyde. He built the house we moved to in Tiftonia after we left St. Elmo.

I never knew the feeling of having a real dad. As a kid, I couldn't understand why it had to be that way. There were stepfathers and others that drifted in and out of our lives, but I knew the relationships were not the real thing – not a true relationship between a father and son. The feeling that someone actually liked or cared about me was strangely absent, much less being able to experience the feeling of truly being loved. At times, I just felt like I was in the way. It was a feeling I got from the way they looked at me.

In my mind, I had come to terms with the fact I was not the son of either of these men, and became reconciled to the fact that I couldn't do anything to change the situation. Such a realization is tough for a seven-year-old, but there it is. To this day, I have a special concern for the children of divorce or for those raised by a single parent.

Roughly halfway through my second-grade year, things started to get completely out of control. One day, Mom took me to John A. Patten Elementary School in Chattanooga and dropped me off. When I got to the front door of the school, it was locked. I can vividly remember turning around and looking for Mom, but she had already driven away. I had to figure out what to do. So, I walked to the gas station where my mom's boyfriend worked. It wasn't far from the school. I don't remember how I knew where he worked. Maybe Mom had bought gas there and I noticed the way she talked to him. He drove me from the gas station to my grandmother's house on O'Leary Street in St. Elmo.

Children don't always receive enough credit for their ability to survive what adults throw at them. Parents too often believe their kids are unaware of situations. Many times, they're wrong about the kids knowing what's going on. I wonder what my grandmother thought when this boyfriend pulled up with me in the car. Did she know what was happening? Was she upset with Mom? When did Mom find out where I was? Did anyone call her? Did she go back to the school at the end of the day and find out the school had been closed all day? If my grandparents had not previously known about our chaotic situation, they certainly did after that eventful day. I never asked Mom about this day; I just never wanted one of my children to have a day like this.

While this confusing scenario continued, I believed that T. Highfield was my dad. I didn't know any better; I did know that Mom was seeing the man who built our house. As a kid, I was self-conscious, thinking I was the only one with a messed-up family life. Like others in similar circumstances, I tried to hide it any way I could. When I was growing up, I thought I was the only one without both a mother and father. All of my cousins had their parents. I know now there were so many others in school sharing such emptiness, pain, and sometimes adult-sized desperation. But we all were hiding the truth from each other – and to some extent, hiding the truth from ourselves as well.

I spent much of my life trying to make things look normal, working on everything from the clothes I wore to the numerous houses I lived in. When we lived on Moore Road, I put up our Christmas tree. It was one of those artificial silver trees with the base that turned. We had red, blue, yellow and green lights that reflected on the tree and as the tree turned on its base, it changed colors. I thought it was something to see. I can still visualize Mom watching me put our tree up. I was in the third grade at the time.

As long as I can remember, I was always trying to make something out of nothing. While on a mission trip to Jamaica with my wife, I witnessed many children trying to do the same thing – make something out of nothing. You could see and feel the pride in these children. We witnessed people in dire poverty, working to improve their lives the best they knew how.

The gnawing feeling when you have something to hide always keeps you on guard and a boy can collect some pretty convincing excuses for his situation. When other boys talked about what their dad did for a living, I told them anything I could think of about mine.

I hated filling out those green information cards at the beginning of the school year. The blank spaces on the green cards were torment. There wasn't any information I wanted to give the school about where my parents worked. This process represented another test of my creativity.

My stepfathers and their jobs seemed to change every year. In two years' time, even my last name changed four different times. It was normal for me to start the school year with one name and a new stepfather, and end it with another name and another stepfather. Can you imagine the stress I felt? I didn't know who I was, or even what my name was. Looking back now, I have to marvel at how much I worried about this and tried to hide it.

Children from dysfunctional families feel enormous social pressure and guilt every day, and this isn't just the pressure of growing up. Today, I know other adults who had difficult home lives while growing up. They agree the pressures of simply being a kid are compounded tremendously when the situation at home is unstable.

The lasting consequences of an unsettled upbringing can complicate lives well into adulthood. Sometimes we can choose to be bitter and take out our anger on innocent people. I know I have. Every fight I got into while in school was because I felt like someone was making fun of my situation. Sometimes I still overreact to things people say, even when I'm sure their comments were not meant the way I interpreted them. There is no escaping the fact that dysfunction shapes your life just as surely as an ideal existence does. In many cases it defines how you see yourself.

However, despite the pain and uncertainty, there are positive aspects to tough situations. They provide you with a built-in incentive to be highly competitive at everything you do, no matter what it is. You simply cannot stand to lose because losing means you are backing up; somehow taking steps backward toward the life you had left behind. You cannot even consider giving up because that would resign you to an unthinkable but familiar fate. At times, you find yourself willing to go for broke, even though the entire situation is not clear. When you've grown up poor, the opportunity to improve is reason enough to go for it.

Today, as I'm finishing this book, I'm being recruited by another financial institution. They want me to manage their main branch in the area. Imagine me, the onetime laborer with no experience at all, managing the main office. They called me because they were told I could do the job.

You know what that means – fake it until you figure it out. Please find the strength to believe your life can be a great one. Maybe it's not today, but it can be tomorrow – or the next day, or the next.

Even if your childhood experiences were difficult, having gone through those situations can give you irrefutable motivation. Although it's often regarded as a curse, adversity can be a *gift*. You begin to realize there is no real "losing" when you're making an effort to improve your life. With every challenge comes an opportunity to gain valuable experience. When you have lived an unsettled life, you don't look at taking a risk as a chance to lose. You look at it as a chance to advance.

The feeling of having to prove yourself – to others and to yourself as well – is a persistent companion. It's an inexplicable sensation to constantly feel that people don't believe you have what it takes. The truth is, they probably don't feel that way at all. It's your imagination doing a number on you.

I have often referred to this outlook on life as an "I can do it regardless" attitude. The drive to succeed pushes you to excel in everything – your job, sports, or whatever you're involved in. I suppose this is why so many successful athletes are from single parent homes. Winning puts you one step further away from a difficult past, a past with many memories that you would like to forget – but never will.

Harsh circumstances often require children to grow up before their time. When they have constantly been thrown into the middle of adult situations and problems, they have no choice but to grow up. By the time I was eight years old, I had seen and heard more than my share of bad things. I knew more than any eight-year-old should.

When I was about that age, Mom told me that I was the head of the house. Why did she put pressure of adulthood on me? What was she feeling that compelled her to imagine an eight-year-old could take on the head of the house role? I have felt this pressure my entire life, and it would take too many words to describe the complexity of such a serious decision. In her mind, Mom was probably trying to make me feel like a little man. Maybe she was wishing I was grown so I could help her more with the things to do around the house. But she was always proud of me and bragged on me to her friends way too much. Parents will find a way to be proud of their children, even if the children aren't doing very well in their lives.

One night after dark, my mom's boyfriend came to the back door. She didn't want him to come into the house. So she yelled at me to get the rifle and bring it to her – as if that were a normal occurrence around our house. Well, the sad truth of the matter is that when I was eight years old, it *was* normal.

I brought the rifle to Mom, knowing we were out of bullets. The boyfriend was looking at me through the screen door as I walked through the kitchen with the rifle. I wanted him to think the gun was loaded. When you close the chamber of a single-shot rifle it makes a certain distinctive sound. So I closed the chamber and cocked the rifle, and then I handed it to Mom.

She was leaning against the screen door. I stood in the kitchen and waited to see what would happen next. The boyfriend took off and never came back. We had bluffed the boyfriend into thinking he was about to get shot. I still have that single-shot, .22-caliber rifle, and plan to give it to one of my children someday.

CHAPTER TWO
ACTION STEPS

- Our home address changed routinely. If you have moved a lot during your life, then you're accustomed to change. This will make you an adaptable person.

- Make a list of all the places you have lived. It will be good for your soul, and the memories will flood back to you. Those who have moved frequently have developed a sense of flexibility that most others do not have and probably do not understand.

- When your life has been tumultuous, you lose your fear of change. Make a list of the things you remember from the places you've lived, both good memories and those that have been hidden in the shadows of your mind for years. You have likely seen and done and felt more than most people will in a lifetime.

- Be thankful that God has chosen to change your life, sometimes seemingly with the wind. Constant change offers freedom to be flexible, a freedom that you're hardly aware of until you're called upon to roll with it.

- The fear that is often associated with constant change has transformed me. I now enjoy the aspects of my life that are changing, even small things like my hobbies or the restaurants where we go out for dinner with friends. Try to do something new and different for a change of pace.

- I enjoy being in sales, and one of the main reasons is the opportunity to meet new people every day of my life. You can learn so much from meeting new people. Say hello to someone you don't know today – it will put a smile on their face and yours.

- When you have lived an unstable life, it teaches you how to cope with adversity and to make the best out of every situation. You learn to adapt and find the simple joys that exist in every day.

- Change teaches all of us to move forward toward the next challenge.

- I have come full circle. My emotions have run the gamut, from not understanding why we were constantly moving, to hating to move, and then to simply wishing we could stay somewhere permanently. Ultimately, the moving has made me adventurous. Now, I'm glad we made our moves. Make a list of the most significant changes that have occurred in your life. How have they impacted you?

CHAPTER THREE

SOME THOUGHTS FOR YOU TO CONSIDER

"We can change our lives. We can do, have, and be exactly what we wish."
Tony Robbins

- *Action. Pursuit. What are you actively pursuing?*
- *Separate your abilities from your disabilities and capitalize on them.*
- *You can win with a losing hand.*
- *The only place where success comes before work is in the dictionary.*
- *A new word to some, a word you don't often hear people say in this high-tech, hands-free, wireless, automatic, automated, entitlement-minded, "I don't have to do that. It's not my job" world we live in: "**WORK**."*
- *Don't worry about what you don't know; use what you do know and soon things will start to change for the better.*
- *Reaching out to people will help you get your mind off yourself. And watch what God does for you.*
- *Encourage as many people as you can and watch how God will encourage you.*
- *What are the chains that are holding you back?*

CHAPTER THREE

SPORTS CAN SET YOU FREE

Don't end your life with regrets – "Woulda's,"
"Shoulda's" and "Coulda's" left undone.
G.H.

Thinking back on my childhood, I really don't know why I gravitated toward playing sports. But somehow I found my way to the sports I was supposed to participate in. And I know without a doubt that sports saved me from a lot of trouble. Participating in sports wasn't easy for me. Getting to and from practice was never easy. But I firmly believe sports were part of God's plan to form me into the man I am today. When I competed and faced obstacles or opposition, I discovered an important principle: God will give you the strength to knock the walls down that are holding you back.

To this day I enjoy almost every sport, but you won't find me hang-gliding or cliff jumping. Sports are supposed to be fun, not kill you. I strongly believe kids should be doing something positive and productive to keep them out of trouble. Sports can do that and so much more; they can set you free. It happened to me. When I started playing sports in junior high school, I developed a sense of belonging and accomplishment that I had never felt before. Once you experience this feeling, you never want to let it go.

One of the most successful coaches in the world is Pat Summitt – she built the University of Tennessee Lady Vols' basketball program. During her final season, Coach Summitt displayed personal courage every day, battling the early onset dementia while continuing to coach and set a positive example for the world to see. She knows a thing or two about kids. She knows her kids are tough, strong-willed, and will fight for something to the bitter end – especially if they know someone really cares for them. When you've been raised in a single parent home, you notice the families of all the kids you grow up with, particularly the parents. They become your role models. When the parental element is missing from your life, you wonder what it would be like to have a dad or mom to do things with.

As I grew up, I took little pieces from each coach and teacher I knew and in the process became the father that I am today. When you are growing up poor and in a single parent home, you wonder what it must feel like to have both a mom and a dad. You would expect there is a real sense of security and comfort in such a home. If you are not so fortunate, you have difficulty understanding why kids who have both parents at home simply don't seem to think much about it.

I understand now that it's because they simply don't know anything different. Why should the question arise in their minds? In a situation such as mine, you are aware of everything your friends have – their houses, their cars, their clothes, and on and on. It's an exercise in futility to compile a list of such things, but you see everything, even the food they have to eat. Such awareness stays with you – forever. Sometimes, even to this day, I have to stop myself from seeing everything through the eyes of a boy raised in poverty, living in a turbulent home environment, someone no one ever expected to make anything of himself. I know this may be difficult to understand. Turning the seeing off is hard to do. Our past may be in the past, but it has a way of continuing to influence our present and our future.

Trying to relax and enjoy a day is hard for me to do. There are times when I realize I'm still trying to get as far away as I can from the trailer I grew up in. It's a never-ending burning desire to achieve something that drives me. My goal is to accomplish enough to free my family and exterminate any doubt that you can succeed if you *want to* badly enough. I want to leave an example of a life filled with proof – proof it's possible to have a life consisting of more good than bad, a life that has been wisely spent and not wasted.

Chapter Three
Action Steps

- Sports changed my life. Whether it's sports or something else you choose to get involved in, you can use the experiences you gained from these activities to help identify the times in your life when you could have tried harder.

- Write down the times in life when you quit or didn't give it your best. Then ask yourself why you quit.

- Write down all the times when you did win. It's worthwhile to remember what you've done well. Write down what you did that enabled you to succeed and why you performed so well at the time. Take a leap of faith in yourself and apply those same skills to your current circumstance.

- Write down all the areas of your life in which you excel. Focus on those areas in which you can achieve an even higher level of excellence. You have the talent to take yourself wherever you want to go.

- Concentrate your efforts today and tomorrow on the areas of your life where you have done well. These are the areas where your skills and talents are directly associated towards your destiny.

- Continually working to improve yourself is one of the most important endeavors of your life. You can change; however, realize that you can never expect others to change for you. Find friends, maybe some new friends, and loved ones who will encourage you to be your best, and then summon the strength within yourself to make the necessary changes.

CHAPTER FOUR

SOME THOUGHTS FOR YOU TO CONSIDER

"Your life does not get better by chance, it gets better by change."
Jim Rohn

- *Big Brothers/Big Sisters showed me what a real family looks like. It doesn't take much to plant a seed that can and will stay with you for a lifetime.*

- *In business they say, "Save yourself first." The only way to do that is to help others do the same.*

- *What do you do with people who do not want to listen to you? Find someone who will. People start listening when the example you are setting is working.*

- *Millionaire investor Warren Buffett said cash is a bad investment, but he also said to keep some around just in case someone tries to get you. Trouble can rear its ugly head at any time.*

- *Quantity has a quality all its own.*

- *Do you shine your shoes once a week?*

- *Do you brush your teeth at least twice a day?*

- *Try standing on your own two feet for a change.*

- *Leave everything you touch better than you found it.*

- *It really doesn't matter who your daddy was.*

CHAPTER FOUR

ME AND BIG BROTHERS-BIG SISTERS

O.P.E. – Other People's Experiences
G.H.

When I was in the third grade at Woodmore Elementary School in 1960, one of the most significant events in my life took place. Mom set aside the time to take me to the Big Brothers Association. This gave me the opportunity to see with my own eyes the way a healthy family could be. This experience left an everlasting impression on my life. The wisdom and foresight she had, to realize how this experience could help me, says to me Mom had the ability to envision how things could be and act upon it, despite the chaos her own life was in.

While we were at the Big Brothers office, the man we met with asked me what I liked to do for fun. A few days later, I met Mr. McKinney. We did a lot of things together and many of them were for the first time. He took me bowling every Tuesday. We built model cars and went hunting, but never killed anything. We just walked and talked. We went to see the movie *Gone with The Wind* in a theater with a wrap-around screen. We sat on the front row. It was a special time in my life. We went to the Tennessee walking horse show and there I was on the front row. Mr. McKinney made sure I was happy and feeling special.

When I was with Mr. McKinney, I knew nothing crazy was going to happen. I felt safe. We did things together for a year. At the end of that year we had our last outing together. He took me home and as we were standing just inside the front door, he told Mom that he wasn't ever coming back. His words sent shock waves through me; I didn't want to hear what he was saying. I didn't want him to leave me. I wanted to stay with him and keep doing all the fun things we did together.

But he had done his job – I had seen the way a normal family could be. As I ran out of the room, I heard Mom say, "He will be all right." He was gone, like a sunny day, and now in my mind it would be dark again. Mr. McKinney had shown me what a family was supposed to be like. I wish I could thank him today for what he did for me. I needed an example of how a dad should act, and he gave it to me. Even though our relationship ended abruptly after a year, I still appreciate what he did. It doesn't take much to make a significant difference in the world of a child. I thank God for the family I have today. God has blessed me with the kind of family I first experienced through Mr. McKinney.

In 2007, I was nominated to the board of directors of the Big Brothers-Big Sisters Association of Chattanooga. Telling Mom that I had been named a member of the board was a heartfelt moment for both of us. The only time I ever talked about Big Brothers-Big Sisters in public, or with anyone, was during a special event held at the convention center of the Chattanooga Choo-Choo a few years ago. The event kicked off the local United Way campaign, with the head coach for the University of Tennessee girls' basketball, Pat Summitt, serving as the guest speaker. I was asked to tell the gathering a little of my story, and until that day not even my family had heard any of the details about my big brother. Kimberly and our daughter, Camellia, were sitting at a table in front of the podium. As I started to share my story with the audience, I became so overwhelmed with emotion, it was almost impossible to speak.

Seeing Kimberly and Camellia sitting there together was more than I could bear. Coach Summitt reached up and held my arm as I was trying to calm down and finish my comments. It was the toughest thing I had ever experienced, and it was in front of two hundred and fifty people. But when the evening was over, as I was walking to my car, people were congratulating me and saying they would like to have heard more of the story. So what Mom did for me really did paid off – and that hadn't happened many times in her life. I know that because of Mr. McKinney, I have been able to be a better dad to my children. Mr. McKinney opened up the door of his life for me, letting me see what is possible. He gave me hope of a better life. I saw that a husband and wife could be happy together. Thank you, Mr. McKinney, wherever you are. Thank you.

This experience brings to light how little it takes to change someone's life forever. It's a priceless feeling to tell someone you understand how it feels to be from a splintered family. The somewhat ironic fact is that the children from single-parent homes may consider the experience the best thing that could happen to them. That's not to say it's a good or desirable thing to be without a mother or a father. However, I'm saying you can make something out of yourself if you want to. And I know being raised in a broken home gives you a keen perception into how the problems get started in the first place. You cannot change the past, but you can surely change the future, forever and always. It's possible.

When bad things are going on around a child, the child often harbors tremendous amounts of confusion and aggression. I was always being put in situations with my mother's boyfriends. Mom was always fighting with them, and she would call me to help her. I only got into one fight with one of her boyfriends, and it's simply God's grace that kept me out of jail. It was God's will I didn't kill someone or get killed. Mom's calls for my intervention went on from the time I was eight years old until after I was married. She was always calling for help. My own kids have no idea what it's like to live in a house with plates of eggs bouncing off the walls at breakfast, or listening to screaming and fighting all night.

One hot summer day my uncles got into a huge fight in my grandmother's backyard. They were holding guns on each other and fighting. It's a miracle no one was ever killed. My uncles, my mom, and her sister and husband were in the backyard. I watched my grandfather walk to the woodshed and get a board. He walked back to where everyone was fighting and hit one of my uncles in the head with the board. My uncle was bleeding badly; his forehead had been sliced open. When my grandmother saw this, she fainted and fell to the ground. My uncle was standing over her, drunk out of his mind, the blood from his head was dripping all over her.

When I saw what was about to happen, I took off through the back door and out the front door of my grandmother's house. I ran up the street to my cousin's house about a quarter of a mile away. As I got to the front

My maternal grandparents, K.C. and Ruby Carlton, are shown at their home where I lived part of the time during my boyhood years.

yard of my uncle's house, I started yelling for my cousin. She ran out the front door onto the front porch. I told her that everyone was fighting and she needed to call the police.

By the time I got back to my grandmother's house, the police were already there. I can't remember who they took to jail or even what happened in the next few hours after the fight. Those visions are gone, never to be recalled. I've seen some horrific things, and I know that some kids have seen much worse. You cannot erase all of the bad memories. Some of them will be with you forever, but it will be okay. This might be your past, but it doesn't have to be your future. There's plenty of time to make many more new memories, ones worth keeping.

CHAPTER FOUR
ACTION STEPS

- Consider the examples from the good people you have known and use them to build a foundation for your life. The examples are there for you to see, but you have to be looking for them.

- Take a good look at successful sports figures. Watch how they respond to difficult circumstances. Take some time and write down the things you have seen them overcome. Then write down how you've responded to your own difficult circumstances. How do you compare?

- The speech I delivered regarding my Big Brothers-Big Sisters experience awakened a desire within me to seek my destiny. Think about similar moments in your life when you were convinced you could achieve something that was important to you. Write down the things that are holding you back. Now, focus on what you want to do. Focus with everything you have. Your brain will begin to figure out how to put everything in place. Allow yourself to picture the series of events. Now, take action. Do not allow feelings of doubt to dissuade you.

- Take any aggression you're holding in and aim it toward your goals. Use every ounce of energy inside to focus your mind. Focus! Focus! Focus!

- Cut off any possibility of going back. Remember that where focus goes, energy goes as well. It really is possible to have your cake and eat it, too.

CHAPTER FIVE

SOME THOUGHTS FOR YOU TO CONSIDER

"To change one's life; start immediately.
Do it flamboyantly. No exceptions."
William James

- *God has not limited what He can do in our lives. We limit what God can do in our lives.*
- *Remember that you cannot change the past, but you can change the future.*
- *Answer this simple question: What could you do if you really tried?*
- *Why not you, and why not right now?*
- *Adversity can strengthen your willpower to succeed.*
- *When you see your destiny for the first time you will never be the same…. And it will haunt you for the rest of your life if you don't do something about it.*
- *Speaker Joel Osteen says, "the enemies will attack you the most when you are the closest to accomplishing your dreams."*
- *What's the difference between, "You will see it when you believe it," and "I will believe it when I see it"?*
- *I'm in it to win it.*
- *Joel Osteen says, "you're the answers to your prayers."*
- *God will give you another chance, so get ready.*
- *Realize how truly amazing you are.*

CHAPTER FIVE

HARD TIMES IN JUNIOR HIGH

"Be bold, and mighty forces will come to your aid."
Basil King

One of the most difficult things in life is trying to make something out of nothing. That's how I would describe my early teen life. It's one thing to have the right resources, the right support, and be in the right place at the right time. But when you're starting off with basically nothing, and little hope of a better life, what do you do? I can attest that things don't just happen to get better for no reason at all – they require effort and hard work.

The easy way out is to blame everyone else for the problems we have. It's much harder to blame ourselves, that's why no one ever does. When you start taking responsibility for your circumstances, your circumstances will start to change. WOW. I can't tell you where I found resolve, but I made a decision I wouldn't let my circumstances control my behavior – or my life. Somewhere along the way I learned a simple truth: Circumstances don't determine your outcomes. You do.

The summer before I started junior high school, Mom was very sick. She had to be hospitalized to help her deal with the things going on in her life. Mom was going through her fifth divorce at the time. I can't imagine the pain of knowing that your life is about to come apart at the seams again.

After moving back to Chattanooga from Cincinnati, Ohio, we moved into a trailer behind my grandmother's house. Mom had lost the ability to think clearly. I don't know all of the details about the divorce. But I do know that stress can do a number on you. Stress can cause you to lose your ability to make sound decisions. It causes you to be confused about everything. Mom was struggling, so our family did what families do – they stepped in and helped her. While she was getting well, I lived with an aunt and uncle for the first couple of months of my seventh grade school year.

During this time, I went out for football and practice was after school. My aunt lived about fifteen miles from my school. Someone had to pick me up after practice, and this added additional stress to an already tenuous situation. My aunt and uncle had their own children and they participated in their own activities. Now they were trying to take care of me, too. My aunt was also trying to help, but their home was not large enough to have a separate bedroom for me to sleep in. After a while it was clear that it was time for me to move somewhere else.

I was a growing boy. One day I was the only one at home, and my aunt had baked a fresh carrot cake. I ate carrot cake all day long, and when my uncle came home from work to find almost all of the cake consumed, that was it. Shortly afterward, I went to live with my grandparents. My uncle must have liked carrot cake as much as I did.

Oh, well, the cake was good! And to this day, unfrosted carrot cake is still my favorite dessert. My aunt was a wonderful cook, and she went to her grave with a secret coconut cake recipe.

My grandmother and grandfather, K.C. and Ruby Carlton, did the best they could to look after me. This was the same grandfather who could settle a backyard disagreement with a two-by-four. However, I know to this day they loved me. They were wholesome, country people who didn't get out much. Neither of them could drive a car, and that made it extremely challenging for me to get around.

At thirteen years of age, I was essentially on my own. There was no one to tell me to do my homework – or even to go to school. There were plenty of times when I thought about running away. I have always wondered what it would be like to hop a train and travel across America while sitting on top of a boxcar. It would have been fun to go back to Long Beach, California, where my cousin lived.

God took care of me during a very challenging time as a young teenager. I was fed, taken care of, loved, and my clothes were washed. How I wish I could see my grandparents today. I know they would love to see the family God has blessed me with. If my grandparents had not stepped in to help me, I probably would have ended up in a foster home. When someone in a family is having marriage problems, it affects everyone in the family.

All the boys in the neighborhood went to school, so I would get up and go to the bus stop and go to school, too. No one ever asked me anything about my family. Somehow, it worked out for me. Something kept me going.

My grandfather was a good man. I spent hours talking with him under the apple tree where he sat every day. We talked about his life growing up and the duck hunting he did to feed his family.

He died while he was watching "Live Wrestling" on television. I had just gotten home from a road trip with my high school wrestling team. He was in his easy chair, and I was sitting next to him, telling him about my two wrestling matches I had won. Alternately, he was looking at me and then looking back at the TV. Suddenly, he fell back in his chair. I jumped up and tried to help him, but it was too late. My grandfather died while I was talking to him.

My grandmother passed about a year and a half later. I came home from my last day of high school and found her lying in the floor beside her bed. I'm not sure whether this means anything, but I have to think that she just didn't want to be in this world any longer without my grandfather. It was never the same after my grandfather passed away.

While I was living with my grandparents, I was still trying to play football. There was no way this was going to work. I had to walk home from practice every day – it was about five miles from school to my grandparents' house. I was getting sick and tired of carrying my books as well as a tenor saxophone home after practice. The saxophone is another story:

When I was thirteen, I decided I wanted to learn to play the tenor saxophone like Boots Randolph. My mom often listened to him play, and I loved the sound of a saxophone. So I played the tenor saxophone in the school band during seventh grade. I stopped playing the instrument after that year, but I'd like to pick it back up again someday.

During those days of walking home from school, I learned there's one very good thing about a tenor saxophone case. I would try to make it all the way home without setting the saxophone down, but could never do it.

When I got tired and needed to stop, I would stop and sit on the side of the road, on top of the saxophone case, to rest.

On one particular stretch of road between home and school there was a prison. It's still there today. I didn't like to walk past the prison fences, topped with razor wire. This part of the walk always frightened me, so I would stop and rest before I started past the prison to avoid stopping and resting in front of it.

Asking someone to help me never entered my mind, but it seems incomprehensible that no one ever stopped to offer me a ride when they saw me walking home every day. It amazes me now when I think about it, but no one ever stopped. When football practice was over, I would begin the trek home. I avoided the parking lot in front of the school. I didn't want anyone to see me walking home.

Somehow, it was embarrassing that there was nobody there to pick me up like the rest of the boys. So I walked through the trees behind the school. Finding the words to express the feelings I had inside in such a harsh situation is difficult. Psychologically I was in a place that no one knew about, and only those who have experienced something similar can truly understand.

After about a month or so, my walk home began to get dark as the summer days turned to fall. I could not beat sundown to my grandparents' house, so I quit the football team. I dreaded walking home in the dark – especially having to go past the prison.

This decision would affect my next few years in junior high school. When I quit the team I became an outcast to the coaches. I can understand how they could feel the way they did. After all, I did quit. When you give up or quit anything, it changes the perception people have of you. From the moment you quit, people can and will categorize, identifying you with the decision you made. You can spend the rest of your lifetime trying to satisfy the world you have what it takes. But I'm convinced the struggles are good for you.

The feeling of losing everything you have is indescribable. It seemed normal not to have a dad, but now Mom was gone, too. I really had no home to go home to, and what little family we had was basically gone. There was nobody to talk to about football practice and how it was going; no father to chat with the coach about how his boy was playing. There was no parent standing on the sidelines watching. It was quite a lonely time for me. I handled every issue that emerged in my life, and there was no adult to step in for anything.

When I reflect on that period of time, it may be that I will never fully understand the impact it had on my life. However, I know that I'm continually challenging myself to prove my worth every day of my life. Actually, the challenge runs the gamut from a steady push to a relentless torment. The prize? Well, for me the ultimate goal is freedom – freedom to do the things *I'm good at doing.*

Truly, there are days when I want to escape the pushing, to be alone and resign from life for a minute. I have tormented myself to succeed in life. Today my life is a daily push toward the goals I have laid down for my life. An old Eastern European proverb maintains that what does not kill you will make you stronger. I believe I'm living proof of that. Through two months of walking home, racing the darkness, I became much stronger, physically and emotionally. The coaches probably thought I quit because I wasn't tough enough to play football, but that wasn't it. Nobody ever asked me why I hadn't been going to practice. When you quit, you're forgotten.

Thousands of children have had similar experiences, and thousands more have lived through situations that were much worse than mine. So many things happen in children's lives, turmoil that others do not see. Only the children themselves know what is really happening in their homes.

We all have the inherent ability to survive and do the best we can with what we have. That's what I'm urging you to do. Take what you have and run with it. I believe if you're reading this book, you already have some idea of what you're good at doing. Go for it! You will be glad you did. Believe it's possible. And not only that it's possible, but that it's possible for you.

To borrow the song phrase, *"One for the money, two for the show, three to get ready, now go cat go!"*

CHAPTER FIVE
ACTION STEPS

- Are you hiding your past? If that's the case, you're not alone. I've hid mine. I didn't want anyone to know anything about my everyday life when I was growing up, and have hidden much of my experience for the better part of my life. Only recently have I begun to open up and talk – even laugh – about some of the insane events that occurred around me. I am asking you to think about opening up a little at a time, to begin to share some of your past with whomever you choose. The exchange has a healing effect that you will not believe. When you share a bit of yourself, it will free you of the burden, the weight you have carried around with you all your life. For me, the most difficult aspect of this was the reaction I sometimes got when I shared an experience. If you look for sympathy, you may not get it. Just share and leave it at that.

- When people hear your story, it tells them you're not afraid to be real. Some people will not respond the way you might think they would. However, it really doesn't matter. Keep opening up. People will benefit from what you have to say – and so will you.

- Most of the time, it's hard for me to open up. I was playing in a tennis tournament and my doubles partner and I introduced ourselves to our opponents. One of them asked me where I went to school. At first, I wondered why in the world he would care what school I went to. "He must have been proud of where he went to school," I thought, and was sure he couldn't wait to tell me. It struck that small, sensitive chord I keep hidden away. So, I answered, *"I went to reform school, and I just got out."* I shouldn't have said that, and I'm sure he didn't mean to denigrate me. I had lapsed into that ugly defensive mode – and he got hit. He didn't ask me any more questions. I thought I had shown him a thing or two. Wrong again!

- It's going to take some work, but you can become the person you **want to** be by applying yourself one day at a time. I'm still working on it, and I've come to terms with the fact that I will *always* be working on it.

- I will become the person I am capable of being – or I'll die trying.

- Even if it takes you a lifetime to get on the right track, it's worth it. What track are you on now?

CHAPTER SIX

SOME THINGS FOR YOU TO CONSIDER

"What are you doing today that will affect
your family 30 or 40 years from now?"
G.H.

- *Don't give up! Don't quit! Don't give in! Don't stop! Don't leave! Don't slow down! Don't let 'em win!*
- *How are your finances looking these days? Do you have a personal financial statement? Is it a personal financial disaster? Are you facing a personal financial emergency, or personal financial problems?*
- *We should all be seeking to do what we ought to do — refusing to accept the status quo — putting one foot in front of the other in pursuit of one's destiny. It's the pursuit, and not the obtaining, that one's soul should focus on.*
- *There is no devil in hell that can stop you if you are determined enough.*
- *I'm challenging you to do all you can right now: Be a person of integrity, of excellence. Are you guilty of not doing your best? Then start doing your best.*
- *God only knows why it has taken me so long to overcome myself.*
- *Albert Einstein said "imagination is more important than knowledge."*
- *Einstein also said, "If you want your children to be successful, read them fairy tales. If you want your children to be very successful, read them even more fairy tales!*

CHAPTER SIX

DESTINED TO BE A SALESMAN

"Run like someone is chasing you."
G.H.

You can stand on your own two feet, and don't let anyone ever tell you otherwise.

Every step you take will bring you closer to the place where you can excel in anything you want to do. It's natural to look at someone else and judge yourself by their success or failures. But you're not them. You can succeed. Can you see your future? It's right there, across the line you've been afraid to cross. I've often wondered, "Why has it taken me so long to let my doubts go." It's not easy, but nothing worthwhile ever is. But that makes it all that much more rewarding to pursue.

I have always been a salesman. When I was in the first grade, I went door-to-door selling pomegranate seeds to our neighbors. To this day, I can remember standing on a front porch, talking to a lady about pomegranate seeds. Do I really believe I was born a salesman? Yes, I do.

We have all been given a measure of talents. Matthew 25:14 tells us that we have abilities, "God has instilled in us from birth." The heartbreaking thing is most of us do not fully utilize our talents unless we figure out what we *want to* do at an early age. And then if we don't figure it out at an early age, we fall for the excuse, "Now I'm too old to do anything." And worst of all, most people never figure it out or let it out – what they really *want to* do.

I believe in life there are trigger events pushing us to try something new. It could be participation in sports, experiences at work, or some catastrophic event that sets the stage for us to intensely start using what God has given us. When you do start to use your talents, there is something you can count on: Fear is always going to be ready to step in and try to stop you from pursuing your dreams. Fear says, "Quick, stop 'em before they can get started. They're trying to become who they really are."

Our talents have been there all along, just waiting to be fully developed, waiting for us to go for it. Your talents are begging for you to release them. You have the key — so turn it!

It's a shame that we often find ourselves in a corner before we become hard-pressed to step up. I've always tried to make things look better — fixing the gullies in our dirt driveway, mowing the grass, or keeping my car clean. When I got my first car I crawled underneath it and painted the bottom of it black to make it look new. The first time I picked up Kimberly to take her out on a date, as she got into my car she said, "Your car is so clean." My reason for this is something of a personal riddle, this insistence on doing things the best I can. Maybe it's the sum of my life experiences that have pushed me forward. Whatever the reason, there it is. Maybe it's simply *"WANT TO."*

"Hey boy, look at that shine!" I will never forget my Uncle Gayle's words of wisdom. He told me no matter what my clothes looked like; I could at the least keep my shoes shined. The advice has served me well for a lifetime. Recently, I passed the advice on to my son, Brian, at a time in his life when I hoped it would serve him well. It has. I once heard a famous person say in an interview that if you were raised poor, you would always feel poor — and I couldn't agree more.

I'm pushing myself to this day, including writing this book, trying to put my life down on paper for you to see, feel and judge. I've never written a book. When I started writing, I just wrote down thoughts on a ledger pad. I believe it's the difference-maker. You just have to start and not stop. Things will come together if you *start* and *believe*. ***And don't quit.***

I cannot spell worth a flip, and can type a blazing one word per minute. I didn't even finish college, but so what? I'm writing this book to tell a bit of my life story, hoping you will grasp the real possibility of digging out of any hellhole you're in — regardless of what it is. I've seen and been subjected to many things in my life that I've yet to discuss with anyone, and I understand others have had to endure much more than I have during their life journeys.

One hot summer day, I was sitting with some friends, each of us astride a bicycle, in the dirt driveway that ran between our property and the cemetery situated next to our trailer. Suddenly, my grandmother ran out the back door with her hands in the air, screaming a horrific death scream that tells you something gruesome has happened. I jumped off my bicycle and ran to see what had happened.

I found my uncle Gayle in the bathroom, lying in a puddle of his own blood. He had put the barrel of a 28-gauge shotgun into his mouth and pulled the trigger. He wasn't dead when I got to him. He was making his last sounds, but his life was over. There was my uncle, his life pouring out of him onto the bathroom floor. The uncle that had taken the time to show me how to box and shine my shoes - he was gone. We would never talk again.

After my uncle's body was taken away, a friend and I cleaned up the bathroom where Uncle Gayle had taken his own life. I didn't want my grandmother to see the death all over the walls, ceiling and floor. She had already endured so much. This was more than anyone should have to face; even a young boy like me.

My friend and I swept the blood and brains into a dustpan. We were not talking, only gagging and trying not to puke while we worked. I spent the next few days painting the bathroom and building a closet for my grandmother. I was trying to change the way the bathroom had looked. I wanted to take away that horrendous shock she must have felt when she saw her son lying on the bathroom floor. Death has a smell all its own. When I get a whiff of the death smell, it instantly takes me back to that horrific day when a man's heart and soul caved in to the pressures of life.

I have always wondered why my mom had such a difficult time with her relationships. How could I have been so fortunate to find my wife, Kimberly? I did, and thank God for her. Kimberly has been the best wife to me and mother to our children that we could ever have. We're a great family, and I have wonderful kids.

My two sons, Neil and Brian, are great dads and husbands, and real men. My sons are also blessed to have found the wives they have who are fantastic moms as well. My daughter, Camellia, is a beautiful mom, and she has her dad wrapped around her finger. When she calls and leaves me a message on my cell phone, I hear that voice and it touches my heart. It makes me so happy that I keep her messages for months. I've kept her last birthday message to me for a year.

Camellia has a great husband and he's a wonderful father to their two children. Kimberly and I are very blessed our children are all with their soul-mates. There's nothing worse than a parent that has a child living in an unpleasant relationship. It's very difficult to be happy if you know your children aren't happy. I sometimes wish all of my children were still ten years old so I could see them all grow up again – the years went by so fast.

Seeing tragedy unfold before your eyes is horrifying, no doubt. But it can make the little things so much more valuable in life. Although it's impossible to entirely let go of the sadness and troubles of a lifetime, these memories also can serve to heighten your awareness of just how good life can be.

CHAPTER SIX
ACTION STEPS

- Think about the things you love to do and write them down.

- Write down the things you fear the most. Then write down why you fear them. I'll bet ninety percent of them are not real.

- Try something new today. Anything will suffice, just try something new.

- Start and don't quit.

- Somehow you must find the strength to believe change is possible.

- Believe there is someone or something special out there waiting for you – so be looking.

CHAPTER SEVEN

SOME THOUGHTS FOR YOU TO CONSIDER

"You are the average of the five people you spend the most time with."
Jim Rohn

- *We were so poor that for a Christmas tree, all we could afford was a limb.*

- *What do you gain when you lose?*

- *It's good to have an "MBA." That's a Major Bank Account.*

- *I would rather pick corn out of puke than sit in an office all day.*

- *Do you have a "Ph.D." working for you? Poor, Hungry, and Driven.*

- *If you never try, you'll never know what could have been.*

- *Act like you know – until you know that you know.*

CHAPTER SEVEN

PhD: Poor, Hungry and Driven

"I don't want to waste any more of my life."
G.H.

There's a simple reality; the world will take as many pieces of you as it can. And at times there's nothing you can do about it. But you can come away from difficult experiences and become a better person, when you face those challenges and don't quit. They can't keep you out!

When I entered the eighth grade, I decided to go out for the wrestling team. I didn't go out for football. I didn't want to walk home anymore, and I felt like the coaches didn't like me anyway. However, our football coaches also happened to coach the wrestling team, and they did everything they could to keep me from making the wrestling team. It didn't work. I wanted to be on the wrestling team. Maybe it was a premonition; it just felt right, so I took a shot.

I wrestled everyone in my weight class. There were six or seven boys, all from the football team. The coaches' attitudes toward me reflected the fact I didn't stick with football. I won all my wrestling matches every day in practice, and the coaches couldn't do anything about it. It was "mano y mano." The coaches worked with every boy I wrestled to help them beat me.

The day before the first match of the season, one of the coaches stopped me in the hall as I was getting on the school bus to go home. He told me that I was on the team and would be starting in the 147-pound weight class. When I got on the bus, going home to the empty trailer, I felt like I had conquered the world, like I had finally accomplished something worthwhile.

Mom worked long hours at the drugstore, so there never was anyone at home when I came home from school. There was no one to tell I had made the team, but I was thrilled. This was the first time in my life that I had ever experienced anything like this. From start to finish, I had consummated something with no help from anyone else. This was mine. They couldn't keep me out.

I knew that by going out for the wrestling team, even though the coaches didn't like me, if I beat everyone they could put in front of me, they would have no choice but to let me on the team. So at an early age I learned that going for it – pursuing a goal with determination – could pay off. I understood it would never be easy, but it was possible.

I had never seen a junior high school wrestling match before the day of my first competition. I was actually a competitor in the first match I ever attended. It was in the school gym with the entire student body watching. This was the most adventurous thing I had ever done, and everybody was yelling their heads off!

I was one of only two boys on our team that did not get pinned that great day. The boy I wrestled got his ear torn some way, and I kept putting him in a headlock. There was blood and a lot of screaming. Of course, back then there was no blood rule to stop the competition, so my match went to the finish.

Until that day, the only wrestling I had ever seen was sitting with my grandmother and grandfather watching the professional version of the sport on TV every Saturday afternoon. I can remember being in the front yard and becoming alarmed by hearing my grandmother scream. I would run into the house to see what was happening. My grandmother would be standing in front of the TV, yelling for her favorite wrestler to do something.

Well, maybe I learned something from watching live wrestling while sitting in front of the TV. I didn't win the match, but everything changed. It seemed as if I had gone from "nobody" to "somebody" in the blink of an eye. Accomplishing the goal of making the wresting team had been the result of going for it and an attitude that I had nothing to lose. I believe the world moves if you move. "For every action, there is an equal and opposite reaction" (Sir Isaac Newton).

That day, on the wrestling mat in Junior High School, was a breakout day for me. Kids who had never spoken, or even taken note of me, were talking to me now. Then at the conclusion of the wrestling season I finished third in the city and county tournament. One other boy and I were the only wrestlers on our team to earn a medal in the season-ending competition.

Strangely enough, at the end of the season none of the coaches even mentioned our wrestling team, our names, or anything about wrestling. I'll never understand why the coaches felt this way. However, it has provided a valuable lesson. Seeking validation from others for a job well-done can be a disappointing endeavor. First, seek God's approval of your effort. It is, in the end, the only thing that will matter. Then the satisfaction of a job well-done will be your reward.

During my entire school athletic career, I never had my father – or any father figure – attend any of my awards banquets. I made certain that would not be the case for my sons, Brian (left) and Neil.

I suppose it's human nature to want to be recognized for your accomplishments. And it does encourage you to do even more when someone takes notice and says, "Hey, you did a good job." One afternoon, when most of the school happened to be in the gym, one of the coaches walked up and handed me a small medal. He mumbled something simple like, "Here's your medal," and shuffled off. It was obvious that this was his way of saying, "We don't like you." At least I was holding the medal I had earned in the city and county tournament, one that I didn't know existed – and no one could take it away.

To this day, I'm mystified as to how adults whose jobs were to act as role models and shapers of character could treat a child in such a way. As a ninth grader, I decided to go out for football again. They didn't give me a helmet to practice in, and I was never given a chance to play in a game, with the exception of two plays at the end of the season. It seemed with the coaches in control I was never going to get a fair chance on the football field.

When wrestling season came around again, the whole cycle repeated itself. The coaches tried their best to find someone who could beat me. Adversity only made me more determined to win. Of course, the coaches wanted one of their favored football players to take first string in my weight class. Each week, the coaches arranged challenge matches to see who would compete as first-string wrestlers for that particular week. During one of those matches, my opponent hit me in the elbow with his fist.

I still won the match. When I asked him why he resorted to an illegal punch, he admitted, "The coach made me do it." I would like to tell that coach today how I felt when I heard those words, and then to ask him how he could justify such an action against a fourteen-year-old kid. I'll never know.

I won the city and county tournament that year, but received no recognition from my coaches. In the finals, I defeated a boy who had been unbeaten the whole season. The morning of the championship match, my coach looked me in the eye and told me I had been able to manhandle the boys I had wrestled in practice, but the opponent in the City and County championship match would be much tougher. He basically said he expected me to lose.

Well, I won the tournament. The next day, the headlines in the sports section of the *Chattanooga News-Free Press* read, "Highfield Manhandles Richie," in bold, black letters.

When a person has that special something, that *"want to,"* others would do well to watch their words. I cannot stand it when an authority figure mistreats an underdog. My oldest son, Neil, once had a high school coach who, in my opinion, mistreated him. He would put him into basketball games with one second left on the clock. This is a young man who had been Most Valuable Player in just about every sport he attempted. Again, I can't understand what causes an individual to treat children this way. Are they jealous – or just plain old mean? This world definitely has its share of cold-blooded people who don't care what they say or do to anyone.

At best, these individuals may be trying to teach a young person a lesson, and it's lessons like these that can make you fight harder for the things you want in life. Not everyone has been mistreated in their lives. But what's important is how we respond to the things that happen to us. At times I have allowed bad treatment to eat me up inside. Conversely, some of the times I'm most proud of are wrapped around negative experiences that were turned into something positive. This has sharpened my focus and given me the will to succeed.

The next time you feel mistreated and someone has taken advantage of your trust or goodwill – or simply attempted to make you feel unworthy – you will see it coming. Be prepared, and stay focused. As someone has said, "You can be bitter – or you can get better." Another wise individual, multimillionaire businessman Ted Turner, asserted, "I wasn't losing. I was just learning how to win."

I was once listening to Turner in an interview, stating he had lost billions of dollars in a single deal. When asked how he viewed that tremendous loss of wealth, he said, "No use to cry over spilled milk." Good advice, I think.

Yes, I was born poor, and it's always good to remember where you came from. It doesn't bother me anymore to tell someone that I was a laborer and hauled scrap metal for twelve years. And it doesn't bother me that I grew up living in a trailer. People judge others by the way they look, and they always will. However, the old, worn-out saying is true: "Never judge a book by its cover." You have to have lived a little to fully understand and appreciate what this means.

CHAPTER SEVEN
ACTION STEPS

- Are you taking some risks? Taking some risks has helped me overcome many things.

- Focus on where you *want to* be, not on where you are.

- Don't spend any more time being bitter, you're better than that.

- If successful people have losses and can move on, so can you.

- The way you look and dress today can and will change. Get to work on you.

- Don't worry about what people will think and say when you start to make some changes.

- You're going to be great.

CHAPTER EIGHT

SOME THINGS FOR YOU TO CONSIDER

"The death of fear is doing what you fear to do."
Sequatchie

- *Quit pushing your customers and start pushing yourself to new heights.*
- *Be a barrier breaker.*
- *Don't make excuses.*
- *The great battle between knowledge and action: It doesn't matter how much you know. The only thing that matters is what you do with it.*
- *Ten New Year's resolutions: Lose Weight. What kind of weight?*
  1. *The weight of holding a grudge.*
  2. *The weight of fear.*
  3. *The weight of "I don't know everything."*
  4. *The weight of your past.*
  5. *The weight of not having enough money.*
  6. *The weight of "no one else has done it."*
  7. *The weight of insecurity.*
  8. *The weight of procrastination.*
  9. *The weight of lack of experience.*
  10. *The weight of going it alone.*
- *Have you dreamed a dream worth living for?*
- *Listen to what your heart is telling you — and believe you're up to the challenge.*

CHAPTER EIGHT

WORKING FOR MONEY

"Destiny is not a matter of chance, it is a matter of choice; it is not a thing to be waited for, it is a thing to be achieved."
W. J. Bryan

Some secrets to success are simple. For instance, learning to do a day's work and getting paid for doing it. Also learning what it means to do a good job. Another secret we'll look at is the effect that change can have on your life. Early in my life, when I changed jobs I was just a kid trying to get by. I hadn't yet learned that it was "time for me to start singing my song."

I began working when I was ten years old, mowing yards every summer of my life. By the time I was twelve, I was also working with my uncle and stepfather. They painted houses; I did whatever they told me to do, from picking up trash to shoveling dirt. I don't remember if I ever got paid. I only remember my uncle showing me how to use a shovel and telling me, "If you hold it close to the blade, you can pick up a lot more." This was one of those lessons you never forget. I worked with my uncle the next summer, painting houses again. It was hard work.

I was paid fifty cents an hour. I learned some valuable lessons, such as how to get to work on time, the concept of working a full day, and what it means to do a man's job.

There's a term I've heard most of my life – "a day's work." I believe it means doing a job and doing it well. There's a feeling you get when you know you have done an honest day's work. It means you didn't slack off, and you started a job and finished it. I hope you know this feeling.

My early working experiences taught me a great deal about getting a job done and doing it right. What would it do for children today to work a forty-hour week every summer from the time they are ten years old? Would it develop character, strength and willpower? It would teach them not to quit when things get hard. They would learn to persevere in spite of difficulties.

I went to work for a construction company the following summer, earning three dollars an hour, six times what I had made with my uncle. (It's ironic, but this was not the last time I would experience an income increase of six times or more. I'll tell you about that in a later chapter.) With this increase in my income, I realized immediately that change could be a good thing.

I was starting to buy my own clothes for school and pay my own way. I learned having the good things in life came at a price, particularly when I bought a pair of Bass Weejun loafers, like all the cool kids wore. I saw what hard work could give a person: brick houses with fireplaces, cars, motorcycles, go-carts, trucks, and good food to eat. These things make an impression on a young man; they create visions of what's possible. Visions of the way I wanted my life to be.

Growing up I ate at my grandmother's house many times. Squirrel for breakfast, and rabbit and dumplings for dinner, were good meals for us. I saw the things that my friends had, and that motivated me to do something meaningful with my life. I wanted to have something, do something, and be somebody. It created a fire in me that will never, ever go out.

The first work I did was with my hands and I kept this up twenty years – way too long. There's a massive difference between doing a job that makes it necessary to take a bath afterward and a job where you only shower before you go to work. I worked as an elevator and escalator installer, helping to put escalators in several new department stores in Chattanooga. That's the kind of work that can get a person killed, and I don't know of anything colder than an elevator shaft in the dead of winter. Someone once said that the only thing you get when you work with your hands is tired; better yet, working your fingers to the bone will get you bony fingers.

Chapter Eight
Action Steps

- Spending summers working did me a lot of good. Have you ever worked in the summer?

- Make a list of the things you've learned from the work you have done.

- I'll bet that from the work you did as a kid, you have used those experiences in your everyday life. Consider how those experiences have made a difference in your life.

- Be proud and thankful someone let you do some real work. If you can, thank that person.

- Think about how the work you did as a kid has affected the life you have today.

- What have you taught your child that's connected to the work you've done in your life? Try teaching something today.

CHAPTER NINE

SOME THINGS FOR YOU TO CONSIDER

"Be a Columbus to whole new continents and worlds within you, opening new channels, not of trade, but of thought."
Henry David Thoreau

- *Doing unpopular things will get you popular results. God has given us everything we need to fulfill the destiny he has placed in us. Philippians 4:13 says, "I can do all things." If you believe in what you're doing, even if no one is supporting your efforts, keep going. God has given you the abilities you need.*

- *All you give is all you get, so give it all that you've got!*

- *When was the last time a sales representative that sold you something called you back?*

- *A sale is made in **every** sales call. Someone sells, and someone buys. (If you're wondering what this means, try reading it again.)*

- *Everything we do has to deal with pleasure or pain.*

My wife, Kimberly, stitched this poem when our children were babies:

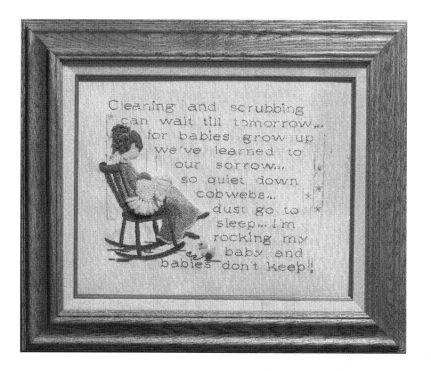

I believe this poem is the foundation that establishes what's most important in any family. Kimberly explained what it means to her:

"There will only be one time in your life to enjoy your children. There will only be one time in your child's life to be a child. Our children are precious gifts from God. Be thankful for each and every day you have in their lives." – Kimberly Highfield

CHAPTER NINE

THE BLONDE WITH HER KEYS LOCKED IN HER CAR

"A woman is like a tea bag...you never know how strong she is until you put her in hot water."
Eleanor Roosevelt

What could be better than a blonde in a pink '57 Chevy? While I was working for the elevator company, I met my first and last wife, Kimberly. We met on Brainerd Road in Chattanooga at a convenience store. My friends and I hung out there because we could play air hockey and foosball – and meet girls. The first time I saw Kimberly, she was "Ooh, La-La!" She had a look that was, quite simply, "It" for me.

Kimberly had locked her keys in her car. I saw this as a chance to talk to her and get her telephone number before I unlocked the car. Now the reason I was so good at unlocking cars probably needs some explaining. I was really good at locking my own keys inside my car; so many times, in fact, that I kept a coat hanger tied under the car. This practice came in handy that day. I go by the old saying, *"Stay ready, and you won't have to get ready when opportunity comes along."*

I knew Kimberly was special the first time I saw her, wearing baby blue hip-hugger jeans and a pink top. She was simply irresistible, and she was not getting away without giving me her seven little numbers. After I got Kimberly's phone number, I found out that she was only sixteen years old, but her friend told me she was going to be seventeen the following week. When I called the next week, she said she would go out with me, but I had to meet her mother and father first. That went well enough, and for the next year and a half we spent a lot of time together.

Meeting Kimberly changed my life at a time when I was not running around with the best crowd. I had dropped out of the University of Tennessee at Chattanooga and quit the wrestling team after receiving an athletic scholarship. I was working and smoking pot. Kimberly was going to Cleveland State Community College, studying accounting and bookkeeping and considering doing some modeling. She had a lot going for her when we met, and would have been great at anything she wanted to do in her life.

Kimberly's enormously intelligent and can see through anything that is going on in our lives today. I consult with her on everything that I do of importance. I've probably driven her crazy at times, asking how she thinks or feels about everything under the sun. But what she thinks is very important to me. When I have gone against what Kimberly thought was best, it has always come back to bite me.

Kimberly has been a wonderful mother, the kind that every child would wish to have. She has also been everything I could have imagined in a wife. She has always set a wonderful example for our children, doing all the things that are important – reading to them, spending time with them, and making the kind of investment that pays off in the long run when you are raising kids.

She's a fantastic cook as well. She has spent many hours in the kitchen teaching our daughter how to cook. My two sons and I have eaten more than our share of thumb-print cookies. Kimberly was the one who insisted we take the children to church, despite being married to someone that once thought what you did on Sunday morning was try to recover from what you had done on Saturday night.

I know God sent me to the convenience store on the day Kimberly and I met, and He sent her there also. We were meant to be together, and we have been together ever since that day. When there is a lot of love between two people, things happen. I guess you could say, "We got married in a fever hotter than a pepper sprout," as the Johnny Cash song goes.

When Kimberly and I got married, I had just been laid off from the elevator company. There we were with a baby on the way, and I had no job. How were we going to live? Out of love for his daughter, Kimberly's father put me to work as a laborer in his steel shop. I didn't have experience at this type of work, so I fit the role of the soon-to-be son-in-law who had no idea what to do on the job. The only other laborer in the shop told me he knew I was there to take his job – grinding and painting steel all day long.

Soon enough, I discovered that my job was to do whatever needed to be done. I was a grinder, painter, deliverer of steel, and whenever we had a load of scrap I would take it to the scrap yard. I mowed the grass and washed the trucks. When the driveway got so rough that it was difficult to drive on, I filled the potholes. When I went to work for the steel company, I made three dollars an hour, half the amount I was making at the elevator company. The baby was coming soon, and I didn't know how we were going to live.

Kimberly's grandmother had passed away just before we were married, and we were given her house to live in. That gift saved us from bringing a child into this world without a home. We lived in that house for twelve years. I worked at the steel shop for nine years before my pay reached six dollars an hour again.

These years illustrate the kind of situation you may find yourself in if you're not willing to try something different. What was I thinking? Why did I continue kidding myself, thinking things would change? I was never going to be a part of what was really happening there. I was working at the steel shop only out of pity. There's a business philosophy out there that some business owners think helps them. They believe it's a good idea to keep some of the employee's "dumb." And if you don't believe this, consider how long you've been doing the same job without any training?

I know that may be hard to take, but it's true. When was the last time your boss or employer tried to improve your skills? They fear competition in the workplace. So they will intentionally hold some people back. What does this mean to you? You have to take matters into your own hands, and it's that simple.

Kimberly and I posed for this photo about six months before we got married in 1974. My hairstyle was a little different back then.

The years added up, and out of frustration, to keep from going mad, I played on two softball teams. We played every other night, and if we were not playing, we were practicing. I did anything I could to release the pent-up energy inside me. When I look back at the situation, the answer was simple. The owner had a son who was going to take over some day. That was obvious. Nothing was going to change that situation. I realized, even then, that I was capable of doing much more than I was permitted to do at the steel shop, but what kind of opportunity was out there? What could I do that would change my family's situation for the better?

I knew I had to find something that paid better – but what? Well, I did. I started hauling scrap. I went to all the body shops at the local car dealerships and asked them to let me have the leftover parts from the cars they had fixed. I struck a deal with them. I would clean up the unusable car parts that were thrown outside the body shop every afternoon. The area would be neat and clean when they came to work the next day. The shop managers liked the idea, and instantly I was in the scrap business.

On the weekends, I would drive through neighborhoods looking for hot water heaters that were left on the side of the street or anything else made of metal that was left for the garbage men to pick up. I would throw it in the back of my truck and keep going. If Kimberly and I were driving on the interstate and I saw a muffler or tailpipe on the roadside, I would stop and pick it up. Although Kimberly didn't like it when I pulled the truck onto the grass in the middle of the highway to pick up a discarded tailpipe, this stuff was like gold to me.

I had lost any inhibitions I might have once had. I didn't care anymore whether someone I knew saw me in the middle of the highway picking up junk. I only knew that I had to do something with every minute of every day. Along with hauling scrap, I painted houses on the weekends. But even that wasn't enough to make a real difference.

One evening, some friends came over and showed us a multi-level marketing program. We could, according to them, get people to work with us and build a business in our spare time. "Spare time!" I thought. "Are your kidding? I have three jobs now!" I wanted more, but there was no more time to work. I had filled twenty-four hours a day with work, and still we could hardly afford to leave the house.

We would eat out once a week after church, and that was it. I remember hearing people at church talk about going on vacation to nice places for a week or two, and they even took trips on spring break. What in the world was spring break? Who goes on a spring break vacation? For me, spring break meant the weather had warmed up and we didn't have to light the kerosene heaters in the shop to keep warm.

I'll tell you who went on "spring break" – people that lived in a world I knew nothing about, that's who. They were the people whose children had alligators on their shirts instead of foxes. I was resigned to the fact, and knew in my heart, that at the shop I would never be more than a laborer or "gopher" – the kind of person that jumps up when they are told to go-fer-this or go-fer-that. Anyone who has done this kind of work understands what a "gopher" is.

When I think about that situation now, I cannot feel anything but stupid for not realizing what it was – a dead-end road in terms of getting a promotion. At the steel shop, I had no chance to be promoted, move up, or get a big raise. I had no way to get ahead, and it had been my fault I had stayed there too long. No one had made me stay. I can't fault anyone but myself for not trying to do something sooner.

I was a hard worker. I didn't lie out, call in sick, or come in late. I tried as hard as I could to be a part of the business. If you are in a similar situation now, consider this: You are a winner, and you know in your heart you're not going anywhere in the job you have now. So for crying out loud, and for heaven's sake, take a chance. An old saying I've come to appreciate goes, "Winners take chances, and pressure is a privilege."

You can choose to be bitter, or you can choose to be better. The choice is all yours. For some reason, I had chosen to remain in a difficult situation, despite feeling extremely bitter and frustrated. It was time to step out, begin utilizing my own abilities, and try to do something about these circumstances.

I never took a lunch box to work at the steel shop. One day, one of the other workers asked me why I didn't bring a lunch box like everybody else did. My answer was simple: "Because I'm not staying here for life." To me, bringing a lunch box meant that I had given up or given in, conceding that I would never do anything else with my life.

There was not anything bad about the kind of work I did at the steel shop. Building things with your hands is very rewarding work. But I wanted more than to just go to work and then return home, day after day. It wasn't for me, and I knew that a laborer's work was the only thing the steel shop promised. I wanted a career, not just a job. I'd had the last of dead-end jobs, and didn't want that anymore. Not this time – I wanted something more. When I came to that fateful conclusion, I had been a laborer for twelve years. I began to think about other possibilities.

Somehow, I knew I was going to be a part of something greater. I just didn't know what yet. That innermost need to accomplish something was burning inside me. Then I had an epiphany, a vision that everything about me had to change. And I do mean *everything,* from a work standpoint. If I was going to get out of the steel shop, I needed to learn some new skills.

Remember to work on yourself as diligently as you do your job. We all know the areas of our lives in which we need to improve. The results will lift you to heights you have never dreamed of reaching. There was never anyone standing over my shoulder, pushing me to do anything differently. The motivation for change came from within.

One of the things I did while out delivering steel was to *take a tape recorder with me* inside the truck. While driving to job sites to make deliveries, I listened to sales tapes that included topics on every aspect of selling and meeting people. I learned how to introduce myself to total strangers. I learned how to start a conversation with someone that I was standing beside in the checkout line at the grocery store. I learned that you can start a conversation with just about anyone if you practice the techniques regularly. I learned that you can get people to talk to you if you ask them about themselves.

So that's what I did. I was relentless. I started conversations everywhere I went. I didn't care what anyone thought anymore. I was practicing on them, and if they would not talk, I would go on to the next person and do it again. I didn't care how stupid I felt. It had to be done. Something told me that if I could conquer speaking to strangers, my life would change. And thank God, it did.

I went to the nearby shopping mall for months. I would walk through the mall and speak to every person I saw. I wanted to learn how to say hello to everyone and anyone I met. I would grin at them, say, "Hi. How are you?" and keep walking. It sounds outrageous, but I would have lost my mind if something in my working life had not changed. I knew that the change had to move from inside me to the outside. I was determined to get over the fear of meeting people. So I started speaking to people every day, everywhere I went.

Whether I was at the gas station or the hardware store, I talked to anyone and everyone until I became great at it; good wasn't good enough. I was determined to change "the condition my condition was in" (to borrow the phrase from an old song) so we could get on to a better life. After doing this for a while, I started going into businesses and asking to speak to the owners. I would tell them that I was working on a project and wanted to talk to them about how they started their businesses and what they considered their secrets to success. I would ask them how long they had been in business and how many hours they worked every week. I was eager to learn everything I could about what it takes to accomplish your dreams.

What could you possibly learn from walking into a business? When I walked into those businesses, I was learning how to unleash my potential and use my willpower to close the gap between a "have" and "have-not" life we were living in. The gap from where I was, and my vision for a successful future, was burning in my mind. This was the massive effort that launched me from the state I was in toward the fulfillment of my destiny. I was looking for my future, fully aware that life was passing me by. I was not going to let that happen anymore. I was intoxicated with the possibilities of the life my family could have.

The people I met were not geniuses. Many of them were living their lives out on a limb. But what I discovered was they totally believed in what they were doing. That was their secret: *Believing, Believing, and Believing some more!* They believed and had faith. When belief and faith are united together, they become a very powerful force.

One day while looking through the autos for sale in the newspaper's classified ads, I had a brainstorm: I decided I would call everyone who had a Mercedes for sale and try to meet them. It seemed logical that if they had a Mercedes for sale, they had something going for them. I wanted to know what they were doing that I was not doing – *so I could start doing it, too.*

I had no intention of buying their car. Sorry. I only wanted to meet them and possibly learn something from them. I took note of how they dressed and what kind of homes they lived in. Sadly in today's times people might think of this kind of personal initiative as suspicious, but all I was seeking to do was learn, to understand what it took to be successful. If there was some kind of secret, I was determined to uncover it and use it for my family. If the answers were blowing in the wind I was going to put up a sail and catch them, somehow.

I wanted to see how the so-called "other half" lived, and it was quite different from the way my family was living. Do you want to know what stood out most? It was that the people I met treated me like I belonged with them. They believed if I was looking at a Mercedes, I must be able to afford a Mercedes, but what I was doing was studying them. It was that easy to break through to the other side. All I had to do was *"want to."*

Believe it or not, some of the people I met while looking at their Mercedes are friends of mine today. A few of them know the real story. I was desperately trying to meet someone who could show me the way out of the rut we were living in. I was also hoping that somehow, sooner or later I would meet a business owner who would see that I had potential and offer me a new life. I was willing to try anything. When I was out looking at a Mercedes, it was not the car that I cared about. It was the opportunity to meet someone important. When I was around these successful people, for a few minutes I felt like one of them. I had managed to enter their world, even if only briefly.

Remember this: Your job is not likely to change. You must change yourself. Talking to people on the telephone effectively is a skill that can be learned. Work on this challenge. The next time you call directory assistance, try to get the operator to talk with you. Say something funny and see what happens. If you can master this one, you will be well on your way to success. I dare you. If you mess up, just hang up – and do it again, and again.

In 58 months I had doggedly introduced myself to *more than 5,000 people*. I had set up 911 face-to-face meetings with strangers. The leadership of any successful company wants to hire employees that actually want to come to work and make a real contribution. Employers are looking for someone who is always searching for ways to improve a process, a service, or a product, as well as an employee who cares about the customer. It's not easy to find individuals who will go out of their way to help someone.

If you're one of these people, and the company where you work does not recognize these attributes in you, then you owe it to your family, yourself, and to God above to use what He has given you – your talents. Find a business where you honestly cannot wait to get to work every day. Please don't do what I did, waiting and hoping for years that something at the steel shop would change. It never will. I can't say this enough. *You're* the one that has to make the change.

Someone somewhere is praying that a talented person like you will walk into their business today or tomorrow and apply for a position. They'll pay you what you're worth and be glad to have you as a part of their team, helping them push that heavy rock up the hill every day. Companies are looking for determined people because you can't teach determination; you have to hire it.

When I finally left the steel shop, I was making seven dollars an hour. It took me twelve years to let go of the "security" I thought I had. Can you imagine being paid $280 a week for 40 hours of work – less than $15,000 a year – and considering that security? There had been plenty of days when I simply wanted to give up. I didn't want to try anymore because nothing was happening. God was not finished polishing me, but I'll admit some days I considered calling it quits.

The following year, as I will explain in greater detail in later chapters, I made $39,000 selling cellular telephones the first year, and the year was almost half over when I started! I worked for just over seven months in my new job that year, earning twenty dollars an hour, nearly three times what I had made in the steel shop after investing twelve years of my life.

Let me use some numbers to show you the difference my willingness to step out of my "comfort zone" made for my family: In twelve years working as a laborer, I calculated that I earned a total of $158,000. My first twelve years in the cell phone business, I received more than one million dollars – $1,000,000 – in compensation. *Did I make a good decision?* As they say, you do the math.

To give you another perspective, consider this scenario: Before I left the steel shop, one of the things we had enjoyed doing as a family was going out to eat after church on Sunday. Although we couldn't really afford it, we went anyway. My children liked to go to a restaurant called Po Folk's. We really did not have the money, and we were actually too "Po" to go to Po Folk's – even when the kids were eating for free!

Why did we live like this? It amazes me to this day. But the fact is there was no way to know that in less than a year we would be able to eat anywhere we wanted, any day of the week. We had applied for food stamps about six months before I resigned from the steel shop. We were told that we made ten dollars a month too much to qualify. That equated to thirty-three cents a day; 33 pennies were all that separated us from what we thought we really needed – *food stamps.*

This, as it turned out, was the last straw – the proverbial blessing in disguise. Scientists tell us it takes an irritation to force an oyster to produce a pearl. I was irritated with myself – more than ever. I didn't know it, but God was preparing me to produce a "pearl."

There's a word that expresses the growth you will experience when you're successfully working on yourself: *Exponential.* We used the word to describe the growth we experienced in the cellular business. The first known use of the word began in the 1704. The definition of "exponential" means massive growth, a ten-x-times increase. That's *exponential.* Your life is about to change exponentially.

CHAPTER NINE
ACTION STEPS

- Don't beat yourself up like I have. Determine never to do that.

- Start believing things will happen for you and they are right around the corner.

- Don't wait for things to change. Be the change agent.

- Don't try to figure out why people do the things they do. You don't have that time to waste.

- You are where you are for a reason – do and be your best while you're there.

- Are you unhappy enough to make the changes you need to make?

- Go to work on yourself. Nobody is going to do it for you.

CHAPTER TEN

SOME THOUGHTS FOR YOU TO CONSIDER

"Make sure what you do is a product of your own conclusion."
Jim Rohn

- *What's the most important thing you need to get done this week?*

- *If you do not feel the heat from the inside, soon you'll feel the heat from the outside.*

- *The ultimate compliment is a referral.*

- *Six ways to have a bad sales month: No calls; no thank-you cards; no follow-up calls; no referrals; no handouts; just sit and wait.*

- *How to ask for referrals? ASK for a referral.*

- *Men, treat your wives well. Take them shopping and get a big bag of popcorn. Just follow behind them and eat the salty popcorn. When you're finished with it, you'll be so thirsty you won't care how much she spent.*

CHAPTER TEN

I'LL TRY ANYTHING

"The mind is like a parachute – it only works when it is open."
Unknown

There are approximately 43,800 minutes in every month. What are you doing with your minutes – are you using some of them to try something new? When's the last time you tried something new? If Kimberly and I had not taken a chance in multi-level marketing, my life would have been quite different. I was twenty-seven years old, playing softball and working at the steel shop. My life was going nowhere. I had to do something constructive with my energy.

When our friends came over one night to show us the Amway business, I saw for the first time a ticket. The Amway business gave me the opportunity to make the extra income my family needed to do the things we had dreamed of doing. They introduced me to motivational books to read and cassette tapes (remember those?) to listen to. The trips we went on and the people we met changed my life forever. Without exception, everyone we met wanted to do better than they were doing.

I would recommend the Amway business to anyone. It can and will teach you what you need to know to succeed in any business. The books they recommended that we read changed the way I thought. For instance, *Think and Grow Rich* by Napoleon Hill jolted me into a mindset I had never known. No one had ever told me that I needed to have a vision. I had never heard the word "goals." I thought goals were the posts you kicked a football through. My "field of vision" was what I had seen through a welding hood.

Goals? What in the world are goals? The dictionary definition is succinct: *"Goals are an end that one strives to attain."* It's not hard to figure out that if you aim at nothing, you'll hit it every time. Now, I was learning how to aim for something that might even have a chance of working out. No one had ever told me I needed to write down my goals – weekly, monthly, quarterly and yearly goals.

Make no mistake. There had been times in my life when I had goals. I just didn't know what they were called. When I was a senior in high school, I wanted to finish the wrestling season undefeated and win every tournament, including the state. I was well on my way with a record of 34-0 when I tore a muscle in my left shoulder during the regional semifinals. It was a crushing blow; and at the time felt like the worst thing I had ever had to deal with.

This was a huge disappointment in my life. All the work that goes into achieving an objective and then it doesn't work out: a tough pill to swallow. My failure to reach this goal still hurts today. But I've learned things happen for a reason. It's a deep cut in your heart, but life has a way of making up for the things that have been lost; especially the ones that hurt the most.

I had met Dan Gable, an Olympic gold medal winner in the 1968 Olympics, while attending a wrestling camp in Pennsylvania. It had been my goal to make the 1972 Olympic team. That injury left a feeling of loss that I have carried with me for a lifetime. As the years have gone by, however, I have used this experience to continue pushing myself when it seemed things were slipping away.

When I entered college, I had the wrestling scholarship in hand, but my shoulder was never the same. It took two years before I was back at full speed; I believed it was too late to start over. I had already left school and was trying to figure out what to do with the rest of my life. I was basically lost.

Before meeting Kimberly, I drank too much, smoked pot, and wasted my days wandering the streets of Chattanooga. I stayed up all night doing nothing. All I thought about was meeting girls and seeing how much I could drink and still drive a car. I discovered that, at least for me, a drunk can see better with one eye shut. Regretfully, that statement tells a lot about where my life and my thinking were at that time. It's only by God's grace that I didn't get in trouble. I was around trouble in some form every day. Some of my friends were selling drugs, and I was fortunate not to have been arrested and jailed along with some of the guys I was around.

There was one exception: I did get into trouble for blowing up mailboxes and was placed on probation for a year. I had to meet with a probation officer monthly. Needless to say, I learned my lesson and never blew up another mailbox.

Getting back to goals, I've seen for myself how goals open up the passageways to dreams coming true. Without goals I feel weak inside. Without goals the pressure of everyday life can overcome my thoughts and focus; like weeds in a garden unattended. Without goals my sense of direction is obstructed and blurred. Goals provide a barrier of protection against the world's constant enticements to go in a different direction.

Goals are like an energy drink. When you write down your goals, it's like putting fruit or vegetables into a food processor. Fruit placed into a processor turns into a concentrated state, releasing energy that would not have been released otherwise. Goals put your thoughts into an intense state of mind.

I believe goals will do for you what fire did for the caveman. When he first encountered it, he must have shouted something like, "FIRE!" After the discovery of fire, nothing was ever the same. And from that moment on, whoever had the fire was the one in charge. Moral of the story – build yourself a big fire, and never let it go out!

Remember the words of the late former Beatle, George Harrison: "If you don't know where you're going any road will get you there."

CHAPTER TEN
ACTION STEPS

- Be willing to consider some new options.

- Start reading some good books.

- Take an assessment: What are the people you are around teaching you? Are they helping you – or holding you back?

- Try to make some new friends, with people who have the life you want for your family.

- Don't watch TV for a day.

- Go somewhere and meet some new friends.

- Decide what you want your life to be. Then, set a simple goal or two that can get you started on the way.

CHAPTER ELEVEN

SOME THOUGHTS FOR YOU TO CONSIDER

"Life is like watching a train go by; it seems to be going on forever and then it's over. Don't get caught watching the train."
G.H.

- *Resolve to be like a rock in the water that forces the flow to go around, creating ripples of new opportunity.*

- *Do we intentionally fail? Is there something inside our minds that tells us we are unworthy?*

- *Get yourself off your mind. Stop trying to help yourself, and go help somebody, anybody.*

- *Don't let fear interfere.*

- *The farmers of Enterprise, Alabama, had a problem with the boll weevil eating their cotton crop. They switched to peanuts, and the diversity saved their local economy. Today, a monument to the boll weevil, an agricultural pest, stands in the center of the city. Change is good.*

- *You can't get up until you've been down.*

- *What will you gain when you lose?*

GOALS: WHAT ARE THEY GOOD FOR?

The Harvard Business School in 1979 asked this question of its new MBA graduates:

"Do you have any Goals?"

These were the responses to that question:

84% had no specific goals at all.
13% had goals, but they were not written down.
3% had clearly written goals and plans to accomplish them.

Ten years later they asked the same graduates how they were doing.

The 13% of the class who had goals but not written down were earning on average twice as much as the 84% who had no goals at all.

On the other hand, the 3% who had their goals written down were earning
*AN AVERAGE OF **TEN** TIMES AS MUCH AS THE OTHER 97%!*

WOW!!!

GOALS DON'T CARE

"Belief is the Rocket Fuel for your Goals"
G.H.

Goals don't care who they're with;
Goals don't care how many of them you have;
Goals don't care what time it is, they're always ready to go.

Goals don't care what day of the month it is;
Goals don't care what you've done or haven't done;
Goals don't care what your age is;
Goals don't care if you're a man or woman or child;
Goals don't care what your education is;
Goals don't care what your religion is;
Goals don't care what race you are.

Goals don't care about how much you know or don't know;
Goals don't care who your mom or dad is;
Goals don't care about the mistakes you've made;
Goals don't care about how many times you have failed.

Goals don't care about where you live;
Goals don't care who you're with;
Goals don't care about the condition you're in;
Goals don't care about what happened before;
Goals don't care about the way it's always been.

Goals don't care about the weather;
Goals don't have any limits or boundaries;
Goals don't care what time it is;
Goals don't quit;
Goals like everyone – even you!

My question to you is this: Why doesn't everyone have some goals?

CHAPTER ELEVEN

CHANGING EVERYTHING

"Sometimes it is not enough to do our best;
we must do what is required."
Winston Churchill

In this chapter I want to suggest some action steps that can help you. I guarantee, if you search for your place in life, you'll find it. **Action** is the key word you need to keep in mind.

It's said whatever the mind can conceive and believe it can achieve. And that means anything! Most people won't change their minds until their circumstances reach rock bottom. Maybe you've been there. Some people are willing to change more quickly than others. It comes down to this: If you are not living where you want to live; if you're not driving the car you want to drive; if your wife isn't driving the car you want her to drive; if you have not taken the trips with your wife and family that you want to take; if you do not eat out where you want to eat; or if your children are not in the schools you want them to attend, then it's decision time.

Are you willing to make the changes that you need to make? How much *"want to"* is in your soul? How hard are you willing to try? How many books will you read, and how many CDs will you listen to while putting forth the best effort possible to improve yourself? Remember, there is no guarantee of immediate success. If you fail at first, keep trying.

Knock on doors. Meet people. Learn from those who have achieved success. How many new people have you met this month? Start asking people for their business cards. If you ask for their cards, in most cases they'll ask for yours. If you're thinking, "I don't have any business card," then get some! There are some excellent sources, particularly on the Internet, for getting nice business cards made inexpensively. All you need is to put your name on them, along with some great quote you can relate to. Maybe you can use one that's included in this book.

We all possess an "it" factor. You simply have to figure out what "it" is for you. I knew I had a lot of work to do before I could even consider trying to get a job in a corporate environment. I began by reading every motivational book I could get my hands on. Then I started looking for something to sell. I didn't know what it was going to be, but I was looking. The key is to always be looking for your place. I believe if you are sincerely working to improve yourself, God will put the right people and the right opportunities in your path. Seek and ye shall find.

I will never know what more I could have been or how much I could have done if I'd been as focused earlier in my life as I am today. Sometimes, however, we simply are not ready to focus. Maybe life hasn't beaten you down enough yet. Your *want to* hasn't turned into *have to* yet. I have a friend who greets me by saying, "How's life beating you?" Not "treating you," but "beating you." For me, the sting of lost opportunity is everpresent – even now.

When I was a younger man, I had failed to see the light and grasp the opportunity to live more fully. All that has changed, and God deserves all the glory for that. As Ephesians 3:20 tells us, "Now to Him who is able to do immeasurably more than all we ask or imagine, according to His power that is at work within us, to Him be the glory in the church and Christ Jesus throughout all generations, forever and ever! Amen."

Chapter Eleven
Action Steps

- Let your mind believe it's possible.

- Believe it's possible for you.

- Decide what you looking for your new life – and go after it.

- Ask God to show you the way.

- We've all have wasted a lot of time. Don't waste any more.

- You have what it takes to make it happen for your family. Do something about it. Now.

CHAPTER TWELVE

SOME THOUGHTS FOR YOU TO CONSIDER

"Just because you fail once doesn't mean you're gonna fail at everything."
Marilyn Monroe

- *God's plans for us are higher than our own. Reach high and stay faithful. When one door closes, God will open another.*

- *I was ready to give up until I was introduced to a few new friends: Matthew, Mark, Luke, John, and James.*

- *Few worthwhile things are accomplished without vision. Without vision, life itself can seem hopeless, with no positive end in sight.*

- *Vision is seeing what can be.*

CHAPTER TWELVE

SUCCESS STORIES AND 'SOMEBODY HELP ME' BOOKS

*"Five years from now you'll be the same except
for the books you read and the people you meet."
Charlie "Tremendous" Jones*

When I became serious about self-improvement, one of my first thoughts was, "Where do I start?" I found the answer in a good book. Actually, lots of good books. We live in a world in which fewer people are reading. We watch TV, play video games, spend time on computers, but many of us choose not to read. But if there is one thing I'd like to impress on you right now, it's my belief in the power of reading. It changed my life forever – and I know it will change yours, too.

It's simple, really. Find a book about people you respect or admire and read it. You'll probably discover they think a lot like you do. Every book you read allows you to take one step up a little higher. Reading will give you some new ideas and help you clarify your thoughts about your goals. To have more, I had to become worth more; I wasn't worth much the way I was.

As I started down the path to improve myself, I became a voracious reader. This was a big change for me. The only reading I had done until then consisted of the latest articles in *Hot Rod* magazine. But when I did start reading about successful individuals, I couldn't stop. It was earth-moving

– for some reason I finally got it. The words were clearing a path for me to follow.

I read books about how to meet people, how to talk to people, and how to introduce myself to people. I read biographies about war heroes. I read success stories about people that had started with nothing and built successful businesses. I read books about people who had been knocked down, picked themselves up, and then started all over again.

The first book that started me in a new life direction was Zig Ziglar's book, *Top Performance*. I had never read words like *motivated, goal-setting, life plan,* and *cold calling.* I felt like I had been living under a rock. I was amazed to realize I had lived more than a quarter century without any knowledge of the fact I could do something better in life by making a few simple changes. I pray I have done a better job in helping my children to understand the importance of self-improvement. I would have done anything to change my family's situation for the better. I was literally consumed with breaking away from my job as a laborer.

The real tragedy of those years I spent without purpose is that I will never get them back. Don't let that happen to you. Don't wait. Begin your concerted effort today to change for the better. Are you working hard to succeed right now? What did you do today that will move you one step closer to a better life?

I could not stop reading and wished that I were a speed-reader to get the information into my head sooner. I adopted what I call the "ant philosophy": Ants work as hard as they can every day, and that's what I did. Proverbs 30:25 reminds us, "Ants are creatures of little strength. Yet, they store up their food in the summer." Ants are thinking about the winter all summer long, instinctively knowing that winter eventually will come. I worked every day to change myself into the person I wanted to be. I knew it was up to me. Nobody was going to do it for me. And you know, I'm thankful they didn't.

I'm convinced that if you stick to the task at hand, you will succeed. Staying with it makes up for what you don't know – until you ultimately get to the point where you *do* know and understand. If you are willing to work as hard as you can until you do know what you're doing, then it won't be too long until you catch up to the people who already know.

Here's the best part: If you keep working as hard as you can, you will eventually pass up the ones who were ahead of you and knew what they were doing before you did. Isn't that the coolest thing? It's hard to lose when you won't eat or sleep or quit until you get what you came for.

When I was in school, I hated to read in class. I would get very nervous and try to read ahead of where the other children were reading, but it never helped. I would always stumble over the words in the books we read in class. Usually the teacher would stop me from reading to get me out of my misery.

I remember in elementary school at the beginning of each year we would be sent to the administrative office to read out loud so they could evaluate our reading skills. I failed every year, and every year I would be placed in a lower grade for reading class.

All the reading I did later in life, however, fixed all of that. I have no trouble reading out loud today, and it doesn't scare me if I'm ever called upon to read something to a group. So my determination to read helped me in many ways – and it will help you, too. You can become a new you.

CHAPTER TWELVE
ACTION STEPS

- Start reading everything you can about the subjects you are interested in.

- Find time to read every day.

- Think about all the time you waste procrastinating.

- Read to your children. They will always remember the times you read to them.

- If you don't have children of your own, find some that would be willing to let you read to them.

- Practice reading out loud. This will help you get used to hearing yourself speak.

- Read in front of a mirror.

- Read to your dog.

- Read to God – He will listen.

- Read, before you go to bed, positive, motivational books and articles, and the thoughts will fill your brain with endless possibilities.

- Read to your wife. She'll probably faint.

- Read to your mom. Or read to your dad.

- Read to someone you don't know.

- Whatever you do read and read and read.

CHAPTER THIRTEEN

SOME THOUGHTS FOR YOU TO CONSIDER

"Things cost too much; no, you just can't afford them."
Jim Rohn

- *What happens when you double a penny every day for 30 days? On day number 1 you will have one cent. But on day 30 you will have $5,368,709.12. This is a very tangible example of what happens if you keep trying.*

- *What would happen if you doubled your effort every day for 30 days?*

- *When you do the math for the penny in the example above, you see that things start slowly — but the results really kick in by the end of the month. So in your quest for self-improvement, hang in there — good things are about to manifest themselves.*

CHAPTER THIRTEEN

LOOKING LIKE A CADILLAC

"The world has to move over, now!"
G.H.

"What you don't know will hurt you." I was almost thirty years old when I heard this statement for the first time. It's sad, but true. Here's the good news – you can learn, no matter how old you are.

The possibilities for a much different life for my family changed when I learned the difference between cotton and polyester. Thirty years of not knowing the difference definitely hurt us. I was trying to improve myself; I wanted to appear successful. In my mind this would change the perceptions people had of me. We usually get what we deserve, and I decided it was time I started looking like I deserved a shot at bettering my lot in life.

As time had passed, I was coming to the realization that changes were needed in every aspect of my life. While working in the steel shop, I had noticed sales reps for various companies would come by and take the owner of our business out to lunch. While they were waiting for the owner to get ready, sometimes they would come out to the shop floor and spend a few minutes in conversation with us. They were always enjoying themselves, kidding around with us and having a good time. These salesmen were dressed for business, and it was clear they wore different clothing than the guys like me who worked in the shop every day. They wore dark or pinstriped suits and dress shoes with a shine, unlike our steel-toed work boots and three layers of long underwear, clothes we put on every day to try to keep warm.

I had noticed the way they dressed before, but on one otherwise ordinary day I became aware of something that had not been readily apparent to me before. These men had freedom – *real* freedom – during the workday. They were able to come and go whenever they wanted, and call on whomever they wanted during business hours. I knew then that freedom was something I had to have. I had to get out of the confines of the shop, and was determined to make it a reality.

On my way home one night from a multi-level marketing event, I noticed a clothing store on Brainerd Road. The road was one of the busiest roads in Chattanooga, lined with shops of various kinds. I became curious, pulled into the parking lot and got out of my car. It was late, close to midnight, and there was no one else around. I walked up to the window and looked at the clothes on display there. The clothes had the look of success.

Of course, I knew that I didn't own any clothes like those in the window, and asked myself out loud, "Well, who wears clothes like that?"

Now, it's important to realize those clothes might not necessarily have meant as much to someone who has always dressed well. If you've had everything you ever wanted to wear given to you all of your life, then it's no big deal. But I had never taken my clothes to a dry cleaning store or had them pressed. I honestly wondered why anyone would take their clothes to a dry cleaner. At the shop, my clothes were delivered by the uniform man, and Kimberly washed everything else I wore.

For someone already experiencing some measure of success, the clothes I saw in the window wouldn't have meant a lot. But for me, someone truly trying to put the pieces of success together, these clothes represented something of a secret that had to be unlocked – something important to be understood. Why was all of this so important? I stopped by that store several more times, after dark, mesmerized by the glow of the lights in the display window and the clothes being displayed. I knew that somehow they represented the gap between the success that could be achieved and the everyday existence I had been enduring on the shop floor.

My motivating factor was simple. If I could buy, own and wear clothes like these, I would be on my way to success – at least with a good, solid start. I had visions of how it would feel being dressed as a professional and talking with other professional people. The visions danced in my head. These were mental images that have stayed with me to this day.

The store was intimidating. It was going to take some measure of courage for me to even open the door and step inside. What kind of reception would I get when I walked in? What questions would they ask me? I didn't know anything about the clothes that were sold there, what to wear, or even what to ask for – and I knew that would be obvious. This might involve an embarrassing moment, but I believed enough in the dream. I had to do it.

One Saturday morning, I cleaned up, drove to the clothing store, and summoning up my courage, went inside. I was going to change. I wanted to see myself in a different light – the light of my dreams.

The storeowner was Bruce Baird. As soon as I walked in, he asked if he could help me. I wondered if he thought I was lost. Maybe he thought I needed directions, or had come to do some work on the building. I mustered up my nerve and said to him, "I do some speaking in front of people from time to time, and I need some help with my clothes."

I had a feeling inside that Bruce took one look at me and wondered where in the world to start. I am sure that I looked like I couldn't afford a pair of socks in his shop. My meager conversation with Bruce began with a description of how the men I went to church with were dressed. I told him that they usually wore light brown pants with a blue sport coat. "What are those pants?" was my honest question.

Bruce walked over to a display and held up a pair of light brown pants. "Do you mean khakis?" he replied. *And there they were.* This was the day that I learned a magic word. I learned what *"khakis"* were. How does that happen? I also learned what a one-hundred percent cotton, pinpoint Oxford cloth shirt is. I was confused at first. Why would anyone want a shirt with pinpoints? And all of my shirts were polyester.

We talked for some time, and Bruce was kind enough to ask if I would like to go home, get the clothes I owned and bring them back for him to look over. How over the top is that? I went back home, gathered all my clothes, and took them to the store for Bruce to render an opinion. Often enough, I would wear a silver shirt with a white tie, or maybe a black shirt with a white tie.

Thinking back on this, I felt sure he could not believe what he was seeing. You get the picture: I was a guy that wore steel-toed boots to work and cowboy boots to church.

Clothier Bruce Baird (left) will always occupy a special place in my heart for his kindness in helping to teach me how to dress for success.

About ninety-nine percent of my clothes were unusable, and Bruce told me not to think about putting those clothes on ever again. I heard someone say once that even if you don't know what a Cadillac looks like, you'll know one when you see it. I wanted to feel like a Cadillac, even if my income was pure pickup truck. This was a life-changing day for me.

Maybe it doesn't sound like much, but it was significant. I learned one of the secrets of the mystifying puzzle of success. You might ask how anything as readily apparent as the right clothes could be a secret. Well, for me it was a big secret because I simply had not been told anything about how to dress. On the rare occasion when Kimberly talked me into going to church on Sunday, I would fasten my only clip-on tie and away I'd go.

You see, no one had ever told me that you need to look the part even if you're not there yet. There's a saying, "Clothes make the man." At least they can help you in making it to where you want to go. Looking the part does help you advance toward your goal, the destiny you're striving to reach. Clothes will help you get inside the front door of the success club because you'll look as if you belong there. I tried to compensate for my lack of experience by dressing as if I had already experienced the success I was dreaming of.

Bruce had shown me how to tie a tie and put the dimple in at the top. I didn't know anything about any of this stuff until that day. I had lived twenty-seven years, and had no clue about how to dress for success.

He also went one step further when he said, "We are about the same height and weight. I'll be right back."

Bruce went to the back of the store and came out with six suits. He said they were the previous year's suits and he was getting new ones. He gave them all to me for pennies. Just like that, I had everything I needed. I was ready to go. Bruce even gave me a pair of shoes he said someone had brought back to the store. Today, he still sells those same shoes, made of shell cordovan leather, for eight hundred dollars a pair.

I left Bruce Baird's store that day with a different feeling than when I entered. He had fixed me up with a pair of khakis and a pair of blue trousers, both of them cuffed, a blue and white one-hundred percent cotton, pinpoint Oxford cloth shirt, some shell cordovan tassel shoes, and a shell cordovan belt. I was a little nervous about wearing shoes with small leather flowers on them. I did check out the men's shoes at church on Sunday to make sure they had some tassels on them.

Bruce altered my life that day and forever after. There is no way I can ever repay him or quantify the impact he made on my life. I believe God puts people in our lives that can help lift us up to the next level. Through Bruce, God changed my life. Bruce didn't have to do what he did for me that day – but he did. Thanks, Bruce, for helping me change my life.

Years later, I asked Bruce why he extended such kindness to a complete stranger. This was his explanation:

"When Gary first came in my store, I saw a young man that knew he wanted to look and feel better about his appearance. I wanted to do all I could to help him achieve his goal. He knew where he wanted to end up, but had no idea how to change to accomplish the finished product. Gary needed guidance to put it all together – and that is what makes my job very rewarding."

Often, we are all so close to the changes we need to make. For me, the secret to success was the simple fact that I had to stop what I was doing and step across the line and *want to* change. I had to venture into Bruce's store, risking the possibility I would be laughed at or made to feel small. Thankfully, he took compassion on a young man that needed a lot of help.

He could tell by looking at me that I didn't know what to ask for. I just knew that something had to change. Regardless of the fact I had no education and no experience, these new clothes would make it look like I had it together. As Mom always said, "Son, fake it till you make it."

I hope you'll share this story with someone that you feel has *"WANT TO"* and needs some encouragement. But make sure they have a lot of this *want to* before you suggest any changes they might *want to* consider making.

There's a saying, "Clothes make the man," but when I began my quest toward self-improvement, I didn't even know what "khakis" were!

To this day, whenever I go into Bruce Baird's store (now located on Broad Street in Chattanooga) to get a shoeshine, I cannot help but remember when I took that first step, through his front door. Learn to dress well. You can learn a lot by reading a book on how to dress for business. Do the best you can with what you have today and invest a dollar and buy a used copy of one of those "how to dress for success" books. It will pay you back a million times. Or better yet, visit the Bruce Baird & Co. store and tell Bruce that Gary Highfield sent you.

One more thing: Be sure to ask Bruce to show you his latest collection of "khakis." They just might do for you what they did for me. I truly hope so.

CHAPTER THIRTEEN
ACTION STEPS

- Look at the successful people you see and imagine yourself looking the way you want to be.

- Spend a dollar and pick up a book on how to dress for success.

- Don't worry how people will react to the new you.

- Be ready to make some new friends.

- Dressing professionally will give you some confidence you haven't had before.

- After you find the best clothing store in your town, go in. They'll be very glad to help you become the person you were meant to be.

- Are you leaving any tracks for your family to follow? I've spent my life trying to leave some tracks for my children. At the end of my tracks, my children can take it from there, leaving their own tracks for their children, and their children's children to follow.

CHAPTER FOURTEEN

SOME THOUGHTS FOR YOU TO CONSIDER

"You only live once, but if you do it right, once is enough."
Mae West

- *Will the roots we leave work in the future? The roots control the branches. How do we nurture the roots that create an environment that will help your children's children?*
- *In Sunday school class one morning, we were discussing the fact that we all sin. Someone said that when we confess our sin it helps us to face the fact that we have and can lose control of our behavior. One man said that at work he was responsible for sanding countertops and sometimes he would sand all the way through the veneer. He said when that happened it was so easy to blame someone else. He had noticed a lot of other people would blame something on someone else. Life is that way. We all look for someone else to blame. Don't play the blame game.*
- *Jesus told Peter to step out of the boat and come to Him. Peter got out of the boat and started to walk on the water. In just a short amount of time, he started to sink. He had taken his eyes off the Lord.*
- *Have you ever had an experience during which you emphatically knew you were not in control?*
- *Have you ever thought about how much of your time is controlled by someone else?*

CHAPTER FOURTEEN

I'VE HAD IT – ENOUGH IS ENOUGH

"My, my, my; what a tragedy to not even try."
G.H.

There are moments in our lives when we become very aware of our circumstances, clearly realizing, "This is it!" We can feel the moment has finally arrived. It's when you know there is no holding back now – it's time to charge head-long into what your life is supposed to be.

This was my moment. I was thoroughly disgusted with myself. I'd had it up to my nose with the "do-without life" we had been living. Enough was enough of this hogwash excuse: "Things cost too much." And here it is, the truth: Things don't cost too much. We just can't afford them. On that day I realized it was time that I started doing something about it.

The obvious first thing to do was decide on a career. Right! Where to start? I knew I wanted to sell something. I had read that sales people were the most highly paid people in the professional/corporate world. I remembered motivational speaker Zig Ziglar had said when his children were deciding what to do with their professional lives, he advised them that he didn't care what they did for a living. In fact, he told them he didn't care what they sold – just as long as they sold something.

Selling puts you in charge of your income. I was a father, working as a laborer, and hadn't received a pay increase in three years. I was thirty-one years old when I told myself, "That's it! As I said, I'd had enough of not having enough income for my family to live comfortably. I was sick of beans and cornbread and continually having to say, "We can't afford it!", "We can't do that!", or "We can't go there!" It was time for me to stop complaining that things cost too much.

The final straw came when we had taken a one-day vacation. I thank God for cultivating inside of me the drive to want to make a change. At the steel shop, we were given one week of vacation per year, and this was the first day of that week. My vacation pay was $165. One hundred and sixty-five dollars! This was for a family that made 33 cents a day too much to qualify for food stamps.

We were on our way to Nashville, Tennessee, to visit an amusement park for the day. Since money was always tight, we were planning to drive the one-hundred and thirty-five miles or so back to Chattanooga in the evening rather than pay for a hotel room in Nashville. Why waste money when we could drive all the way back home after spending one day at the park, right? Have you ever done that? We were living the life of Po' Folk.

En route to the park, we stopped at a restaurant for breakfast and ate at the buffet because two of the kids were young enough to eat free. Breakfast still cost us thirty dollars. A full tank of gas cost another twenty dollars. Our tickets to the park cost seventy-two dollars. Before we had gotten through the gate to the park, I was down to forty-three dollars. We would need to eat lunch and then decide whether there was enough money left for dinner. There wasn't.

Does this ring a bell with you? It makes you want to beat your head against a wall, doesn't it? We ate ice cream and cotton candy for lunch in the park, and as daylight was fading we headed toward the exit. We stopped at a small rollercoaster so that Neil, Brian and Camellia could have one last ride before we reached the parking lot. As they were riding, they laughed and smiled. I knew they were happy, two brothers and their little sister sitting together and having fun.

Yes, the children were happy, but I certainly was not. Anger smoldered inside me, and it erupted like an atomic bomb. I was mad as hell at myself. This was not the way I wanted us to live. We were all thirsty, so I bought *one lemonade* for all of us to share. That was all I could afford. Then we headed back home. The old declaration, "That's it!" was never truer for me. However, something was different when I said it this time. I had less than five dollars in my pocket and half a tank of gas. I decided then and there, this was my last "That's it!"

In the darkened car, with the children asleep in the backseat, I knew I had to do something. I had to find a way out of this nowhere existence. Once again I determined that we weren't going to live like this any longer. The next day I got up and walked next door and started painting my next-door neighbor's house. This was the last house I intended to paint – and there would be no more trips to the scrap yard. Are you living like this now? Stop right now and make a decision to do whatever it takes to fix it.

CHAPTER FOURTEEN
ACTION STEPS

- Decide what makes you happy. If you enjoy what you do to make a living, you will never work a day of your life.

- Decide the life you want for your family.

- Do you know in your heart that you are holding back, afraid to step out and take a chance?

- How long are you willing to let your family do without?

- Make a decision today, and tomorrow will change.

- If you don't know where to start, then throw a rock. Go to the rock and start there. If you encounter someone along the way, start a conversation and see where that goes.

- What do you say to that person? Simply state that you're the next person after that rock. That will certainly get a conversation started.

CHAPTER FIFTEEN

SOME THOUGHTS FOR YOU TO CONSIDER

"Everything you can imagine is real."
Pablo Picasso

- *Shoot for the stars. Who knows, you may hit the moon.*

- *Are you doing your best?*

- *The importance of having a plan can never be overlooked. We must develop a plan that will take us forward. We must start figuring out how to do it — and stop figuring out how NOT to do it.*

- *Abraham Lincoln said, "What are we, and where are we going?"*

- *I challenge you to stop seeing yourself the way you **are** and start seeing yourself the way you **can be**.*

- *We grow the most when we are tested. The times when we are unsure, but go ahead anyway, are the times when we learn the most.*

CHAPTER FIFTEEN

I HAVE NO BACKUP PLAN

"Limits end when visions begin."
G.H.

It was time for me to take my foot off of first base. There would be no more holding on or turning back for me. No more playing it safe, or over-thinking about what I should do. I finally knew what to do – and it was time for me to do it.

When I went back to work at the steel shop after a long week of painting my neighbor's house and a lot of soul searching, I knew my days as a laborer were numbered.

One day in the steel shop, I picked up a piece of three-quarter inch lime-stone gravel that had been on the dirt floor for twenty five years. Every time we painted steel, the gravel had also gotten painted, and it had become as big as a walnut. I took the gravel to the table where I worked and smashed it with a three-pound hammer. It cracked open like a nut. I could see the rings of paint that had accumulated over the twenty-five years, layer upon layer.

Looking at it, I realized my existence was similar to that of the gravel. The rings of paint epitomized the years of my life I had spent working in the steel shop. I was getting out of there.

When the brain conceptualizes an idea, the body and spirit are set into motion. Go with the visions you have in your mind's eye, the ones you can see with your eyes closed. But be ready. Doubt will rear its ugly head; doing everything it can to drain your strength and mightily testing your resolve.

Fear of the unknown has paralyzed many an individual who intended to make a major life change. I'm talking about the kind of change that will propel you forward, leaving behind a life of daily survival and barely scraping by as a family. This is change that will enable you to give your children the life they deserve.

I worked for ninety more days at the steel shop. On December 1, 1985, I waited until quitting time, when the owner would usually come out of his office and stand on the sidewalk in front of the shop. *My world – and my family's world – was both about to change forever.* I was earning seven dollars an hour, supporting a wife and three children. I asked for a dollar per hour pay increase. The answer was a resounding, "No!" I thank God every day for that no!

Really, it was what I expected, and I had mentally prepared for the negative response. I had also committed to take immediate action. Any doubt about what I had to do was obliterated from my mind. After all the years of working at the steel shop, there would be no excuses to keep me from moving forward this time.

I gave a month's notice. The day before Christmas was my last day as a laborer, scrap hauler, house painter, grass cutter, delivery boy, pothole fixer, truck driver, and truck washer. I had made up my mind I was going to sell something. *I didn't know what, and didn't care what,* but I was going to forge a career in sales.

Of course, people are often free with their opinions. If I heard it once, I heard it a thousand times: You're crazy to leave the "great job" at the steel shop to take a chance in sales. There was no guarantee of success in sales, and I was leaving a guaranteed seven dollars an hour – a "very safe" seven dollars an hour!

I reasoned, however, that the return on the investment would be more than equal to the risk; and *I was willing to take it.* For twelve years I had only been allowed to do the most elementary jobs in the steel shop. When I finally taught myself how to weld, I built belt guards for eleven years. That would be as monotonous as digging holes every day for eleven years. During my last month at the shop, I told the owner that I was not going to build any more belt guards. I wanted to build something more challenging; I asked to build handrails. The owner became so upset he threw the blueprints out the back door of the shop, onto the gravels that lay in the floor. I walked over and picked up the blueprints, and proceeded to build handrails. I built handrails for a month. I sanded, painted and delivered the handrails.

Building the handrails in those final days proved to me I could have and should have been doing something more challenging and rewarding all along. None of those rails were ever returned as defective.

Just for the record, the shop had never been a place for anyone who was afraid of a hard day's work. In the wintertime, it was so cold that the soft drinks delivered by the route man would freeze and explode. We actually had to put them in the refrigerator to keep them from freezing. From one extreme to the other, it was sweltering hot in the summertime and blistering cold in the winter.

I thank God every day that I did not get the dollar raise, and also thank God for giving me the will to move on and use the talents He had given me. I shudder to think where I would be today, and where my family would be, if I had gotten the one-dollar raise. Thank God! Thank God that I didn't get that dollar!

My old steel-toed work boots, worn virtually to the nub, strike quite a contrast to the first pair of Alden dress shoes I acquired at Bruce Baird's clothing store.

The thought of becoming an overnight sensation vanished rapidly with my first sales job. It was short lived. A friend asked me to be the salesman for his company selling church directories only a few days after I had resigned from the steel shop. Church directories were, and still are, big business in the South, where it seems there's a church on every corner. The families of a particular church are invited to have their photos made for inclusion in the directory. They receive a free 8x10 family photo and a copy of the directory and are invited to purchase other photos from the sitting.

I was not a photographer, but we practiced with the equipment for a few days and off I went. Undaunted, I began calling on large churches with five hundred or more members. I would schedule a meeting with the ministers and offer a new directory in exchange for the opportunity to sell portraits to their members. I arranged times for families to have their photos taken, and then a time for them to come back and view them. I made seventy-plus face-to-face calls on churches in the next ninety days, and managed to close a half a dozen deals.

But the four owners decided to fire me and take over the sales and picture-taking themselves. I was making it look too easy. They figured they didn't need me to sell the directories, reasoning they sold themselves. They were wrong, but at least I wasn't welding anymore and had proved to myself that I could do something different. I had broken free from the laborer job, and despite this early setback, I was doggedly determined to keep pushing forward.

I know that I received three specific gifts from God. You might not consider them gifts at first. I didn't either. But soon I hope you'll feel as I do today. Because they truly were gifts, gifts that pushed my family and me to a new and better life:

- The first one was not qualifying for food stamps. We made thirty-three cents a day too much to get the stamps.
- The second was not receiving the one-dollar raise, even though I had not received a raise in years.
- The third was being fired from my first sales position.

I thank God for all three of these gifts. These gifts changed everything.

Why do I consider these "gifts," not receiving what I had felt I and my family needed and deserved? Think about it for a minute. If I had gotten the food stamps, considering the dire financial shape we were in, it would have made a huge difference for my family. At the time, it would have added about four hundred dollars of free food to our table. That would have seemed gigantic for us.

Getting a dollar raise would have added another two hundred dollars to our monthly income, and it was desperately needed. And if I had not gotten fired from my first sales position, I know I would have sold a lot of church directories, but I might have missed out on another opportunity I was soon to discover.

Here's the point: If we had gotten any of these, I may have been satisfied with what I received. I might have been willing to settle for a little crumb of what life has to offer. I may have climbed back down the ladder of life. I may have settled for a penny when life was offering up the world. I thank God every day for my three gifts, even though they certainly didn't seem like gifts at the time.

My question for you is, "What *gifts* have *you* been given?" Sometimes *not* receiving what you think you need can be the greatest gift of all. Receive them with open arms. It's God's way of pushing you forward into the new life that awaits you. Don't make it wait any longer!

CHAPTER FIFTEEN
ACTION STEPS

- Enlarge your vision right now.

- Confess to God your belief in what He can do.

- Open yourself up to what God has in store for you.

- Ask God for wisdom.

- Receive His gifts for you – even when they don't seem like gifts at the time.

- Don't make your family do without any longer.

- Accept and enjoy the changes.

CHAPTER SIXTEEN

SOME THOUGHTS FOR YOU TO CONSIDER

"Life is a dream, realize it
Life is a game, play it
Life is a struggle, accept it
Life is luck, make it
Life is an adventure, dare it."
Mother Teresa

- *You must encourage yourself, because you can talk yourself out of something and allow yourself to be brought down.*
- *Anything can be turned around for the better.*
- *To have faith, you must have hope. You would not be alive today if God didn't have another mountain for you to climb.*
- *Every day, forgive anyone and everyone that did you wrong that day and the day before.*
- *Evangelist and author Joel Osteen says we are victors, not victims.*
- *Persistence neutralizes resistance.*

CHAPTER SIXTEEN

REJECTION, REJECTION, REJECTION

"Do something – until something happens."
G.H.

You'll always remember your past. You can't erase it. There are valuable lessons that can be taken and used from it. But you can't let your past become an obstacle inhibiting you from becoming the person you were born to be.

Here's an important question I'd like you consider: What in the world are you waiting for? I've had six friends leave the earth this year. Talk about a sign, a powerful reminder of how quickly your life can pass. It's time to get rolling!

This year a man did something that had never been done before. He jumped; he was willing to jump out of an aircraft from 24 miles in space – just to prove it could be done – and he landed on his feet. If he was willing to take a leap like that, don't you feel strongly enough to jump into the opportunities that are waiting for you?

To become something more, you have to become worth more. What are you willing to do to multiply your income, to see it grow six or seven times? You can do it, but it can't be done in a single day. You know better than that. Like learning to walk, it requires taking that first single step, then a second and then a third. If you have ever considered the possibility of changing your occupations now's the time.

There is always some reason to feel you're not good enough. Companies that are hiring corporate salespeople are not looking for former laborers to fill those positions. To obtain a corporate job, one of the first items a successful applicant needs is a résumé.

Sounding kind of like Rocky Balboa, I asked, "Yo, Kimberly, what's a rez-za-may?" She explained a résumé is a kind of letter that details a person's work experience so the prospective employer can decide whether the applicant is qualified to do the job they've applied for. What are the chances a laborer, scrap hauler and house painter might have a current résumé on hand? *I had never even heard the word before.*

I only wanted to fill out an application and talk to someone. That seemed logical to me – it's the way I had gotten every other job I had held. I couldn't imagine what difference a résumé would make. And besides who would make a hiring decision by looking at a stupid piece of paper? At the time it seemed like a lot of work for nothing. It's a valuable tool but we put entirely too much emphasis into the information than we should. Face to face tells the true story and it always will.

Kimberly did her best to type a résumé for me. But she didn't have much to work with. I had only worked in sales for a couple of months. There were no real results to discuss, no bullet points, no sales training, no computer skills. Thank goodness there were no background checks, since I had blown up those mailboxes some years back and made the front page of the local newspaper. My formal education consisted only of a high school diploma, and a year and a half of college at the University of Tennessee at Chattanooga.

My résumé contained nothing that would indicate to an interviewer that I was the salesperson their company was looking for. (I never thought to add to my résumé the 911 cold calls that I had made and documented in a spiral notebook as I was preparing to make this major change in my life.) No worries, I knew what I wanted to do: I was wide awake and determined to sell cellular telephones – some way, somehow, even if it hair-lipped the king. I had seen an advertisement for cellular phones in a magazine called The *Robb Report*; I sensed this was my ticket to a new life. I took my résumé to the Cellular One office and dropped it off.

I knew my résumé was not impressive, so I acted out of pure instinct. I went back to the Cellular One office and asked for the name of the person that would be looking at my résumé. Then I called the office because I knew no one would be calling me. Why would they? I used a sales tactic I had learned from Amway: I asked for an appointment with that person. It didn't dawn on me to ask if they were hiring; I just wanted to go to work, period. I never gave it a thought!

It's significant to point out that *whatever* it took to get the appointment was my mindset. I was willing to sleep on the sidewalk if I had to – I wanted this job! At times I doubted myself and hesitated, allowing that small voice to start talking me out of what I knew was right. When Kimberly saw my enthusiasm wane, she would simply say, *"If you're not going to do it, then quit talking about it and shut up."* God, I love that woman. We have choices to make in life, and choosing to do nothing will produce results of its own – but usually not what anyone wants or needs.

I succeeded in getting an interview with Harry Hudson, the general manager of Cellular One in Chattanooga. When I walked into his office, he had my résumé in his hand. I knew there was nothing of great substance written on it, and this was the first interview of my life. I could see by the look on Harry's face that he believed this was a waste of his time. I knew in my heart that I had to make something happen. I went into "survival mode." I'd been in that mode my entire life and was painfully used to it.

Harry asked me a few questions, and that was the end of the interview. All he said was, "Thanks for coming in." We all know what that means: "Don't call us, we'll call you." I went home feeling total dejection, with no good news for Kimberly. I thought, "God, I need this now."

I went back to the Cellular One office a few days later just to see if anything had changed. They basically gave me the same answer, this time from Harry's assistant: "We are not hiring. We have no openings." What she said went in one ear and out the other. Her "Sorry, Charlie" assertiveness was not going to discourage me. I had three hungry kids at home!

Another week went by, so I drove back to the Cellular One office. No one had called me. I was just hoping somehow this life-changing door would miraculously open; maybe someone had quit or died. This time I was told I couldn't see Harry. He was busy, and it was readily apparent his assistant was displeased I had come back yet again to see him without an appointment. It was time for a desperate gamble.

Harry's assistant was keeping an eye out for me, and Harry was not calling me. So I called the Cellular One office and asked what time they opened and approximately what time Harry arrived in the morning. The office opened at eight a.m., and for the fourth time in a month I drove back to the office. It was seven in the morning as I sat in my truck with my suit on, waiting for Harry to arrive. About half an hour later, he drove into the parking lot.

I had backed my three-quarter ton pickup truck against the curb on the rear side of the parking lot so I could see Harry drive up. I didn't want him to see my pickup truck and jump to some conclusion because of what I was driving. When Harry got out of his car and started toward the building, I got out of my truck, knowing I had to get to him before he got inside.

Can you picture this scene? If he had gotten inside ahead of me, it would have been game over. I would never get a chance to talk to him again. As he turned the key to the front door, I walked up and offered to shake his hand. "What are you doing here?" he said, as only Harry could deliver such a phrase. We walked inside. I walked with Harry around to the different offices as he turned on lights and unlocked doors. He didn't tell me to leave. Imagine that!

We walked to his office, and he sat down behind his large executive desk. I took a seat in one of the two chairs that are always in front of an executive's desk. Can you hear my heart beating? Can you picture yourself there in the seat? Your mind trying to pull together the right words to say, words that would open the door of opportunity? I was only thirty seconds away from God moving a mighty big mountain. I leaned into the front of Harry's desk, looked him in the eyes and said, "Look, I have three little kids and all I want is a shot at doing this. I know I can do it. I have no doubt in my mind, I can do this." That was all I said. I took what was in my heart and laid it on his desk.

Nothing came out of his mouth. He just stared at me through a pair of crazy glasses that he wore, the kind that made his eyes look big from the other side. It felt as if the life was running out of me. My heart was pounding, but there was nothing but total silence in the air. Five seconds to go!

Finally, finally, Mr. Hudson stood up and said, "Okay, follow me." We walked down the hall to the back of the offices and into the sales department. He turned on the lights and said the three words I'd been waiting to hear: *"There's your cubicle.* There's a phone book in the drawer, and you need to see my assistant to fill out your paperwork."

Harry took a couple of steps and turned around. "One more thing," he added. "By the way, you're on ninety days probation. You have ninety days to figure it out." He left the sales area and that was it. I was in.

The date was May 15, 1986. Looking back, it is amazing how a person can instantly forget how hard it was to get where they wanted to go once they have gotten there. I had felt like I was going to die one minute, then suddenly the dream had come true and the struggle was over. *I was in! I was in!*

I had prayed to God for a sales job and I didn't care what it was. What he gave me was a sales job selling one of the most exciting products the world had ever seen. What an awesome God. There are lyrics to a song that describe the feeling, "It's a new dawn, it's a new day, and it's a new life" for my family and me. Thank God, thank God.

I'd like to close this chapter by giving a simple suggestion:

Lean into the struggles you're having, look them in the eye, and be a man or woman.

CHAPTER SIXTEEN
ACTION STEPS

- When you intentionally and deliberately make up your mind, people will say yes to you when they didn't intend to.

- You can't spend any time worrying about what you don't know.

- The most important thing to do is take action – massive action.

- Let your instincts guide you to the next step.

- Don't be afraid to ask. Asking has a power all its own.

- Don't be concerned about how many times you ask. Keep asking.

- Your survival mode is very rarely used. Try using it today before it is too late.

- I'm sure you've written down your goals by now. If you haven't, get with it!

MY 'RÉSUMÉ'

The résumé that follows is the exact document that Harry Hudson held in his hand the first time I met him. It's included here because I felt it was important for you to understand the desperate situation I was in that day.

Kimberly did her best to type it for me, but she had never done a résumé before this. I had to have it right then, and my usually impatient personality pushed her to finish it. I didn't give her any time to check spelling or look it over for any changes that needed to be made. I didn't care about that. I had to have a résumé to talk to someone, so I gave them one.

I could not believe someone would decide whether or not I was the right person for a job just by looking at a piece of paper. I wanted to talk about how many telephones I could sell and how much I would be paid for selling them.

We have become a lazy, impersonal society in many ways. It concerns me that employment decisions are being made every day by looking at a piece of paper. It's laziness, that's all it is. Oh, sure – we can't afford to bring in everyone that sends in a résumé. But can we afford not to?

Persevere. Refuse to give up, and don't let a small bump in the road prevent you from doing what's in your heart.

Turn the page and you'll see my "résumé." If you laugh, it's okay:

You call this a 'Resume'?

(Below is my first full resume, exactly as it appeared.)

OBJECTIVE: SALES REPRESENTATIVE

EXPERIENCE: HAVE BEEN AN PART TIME AMWAY
DISTRIBUTOR SINCE NOVEMBER 1979. I HAVE
BEEN VERY SUCCESSFUL SELLING SECURITY
SYSTEMS. I ALSO HAVE REGULAR CUSTOMERS I
CALL ON REGULARY EACH MONTH FOR CLEANING
AND PERSONAL CARE PRODUCTS. I WON A TRIP
TO NASSAU, IN 1981 FOR HAVING CALLED ON
THE MOST CUSTOMERS AND HAVING THE MOST
SELL IN OUR GROUP WITH ABOUT 300 PEOPLE IN
THE COMPETION FROM ALASKA TO FLORIDA.

I WAS EMPLOYED BY HERITAGE PORTRIATS IN
JANUARY 1986. I HAVE MADE THE SELL TO THE
CHURCHES FOR CHURCH DIRECTORIES, TOOK
THE PICTURES, AND MADE THE SELL OF THE
PICTURES TO THE INDIVIUAL FAMILIES.

EDUCATION: JUNE 1971-JUNE 1972 I
ATTENDED THE UNIVERSITY OF TENNESSEE
AT CHATTANOOGA. COMPLETED COURSES IN
BUSINESS AND PSYCHOLOGY.

CHAPTER SEVENTEEN

SOME THOUGHTS FOR YOU TO CONSIDER

*"When you reach the end of your rope,
tie a knot in it and hang on."*
Thomas Jefferson

- *Joel Osteen says that God usually works the most when we see and feel it the least.*

- *God has an assignment for you.*

- *Sometimes God uses the most difficult circumstances to set us on a new course for our lives.*

- *Get a vision for what could be.*

- *You already have what you need inside you to do anything you can believe.*

- *Ask God to bring forth whatever is inside you in order for you to go forward toward your destiny.*

WHY A REVOLUTION?

I had to start a revolution.

Why would I compare changing my life to starting a revolution? There are two definitions of the word, "revolution." One describes the circling or orbiting of one planet to another. The other definition concerns a group of individuals, resolved to change their circumstances. Some people may feel you can't have a revolution without having a war.

My life was the combination of both definitions. I was going in circles, meaning I was going nowhere, so I became determined to start a revolution with myself. I was about to do battle with every fear I had that was holding me back. I believe people have started personal, inner revolutions because they were fed up with being told what they should do and when to do it. Don't you find it peculiar and miraculous how people that hardly know you can say with confidence what you should do or "you can't do that"?

When someone is trying to convince you about anything, I believe you should first consider the source. When it comes down to it, they may or may not mean well. If you've ever been told you can't do something, think about where that opinion came from. Were they trying to help you, or to hold you back?

When you start your revolution of change, you are going to make some people very uncomfortable. No one wants to be left in the dust. But the train is leaving the station and it's hard to stop a train. And **you're the train:** You're about to be making some noise and things are going to start breaking. You're going to break the hearts of all those people that said you would never make it. Maybe they're the one's that said, "You're just like your father and he never amounted to anything." Or maybe they're the ones that said, "You can't do that. You don't have any experience."

Everyone deserves a life don't they? Obviously, they do. Be sure to send a postcard to your staunchest, most vocal non-supporters, if you feel the need. They'll remember what they said to you, and having them know they were wrong will be gratifying enough.

CHAPTER SEVENTEEN

THERE IS SOMETHING SPECIAL ABOUT BEING THE UNDERDOG

"Some will be left behind; and some will fall far behind."
G.H.

I can't emphasize enough the importance of *staying ready,* so you won't have to *get ready* when your opportunity presents itself to you. Working day after day and seeing nothing change is hard. It will be a test, no doubt about it. But keep in mind, the perseverance is worth it. One day you will say, "At last!" Then you will leave behind the people who lacked the determination to step out as you have, along with those that tried to discourage you, saying you couldn't do it. You'll prove to them you could do it, because you'll be doing exactly what you set out to do.

Everything I had learned from listening to tapes and reading sales and motivational books was about to be put into action. In 1986, cellular phones were a new technology. Almost one hundred percent of the time our sales calls were the first time anyone had contacted the company to discuss communicating with cellular technology. The words "cellular," "airtime," "access fee," and "hands-free" were a new lexicon. A brand-new business communications vocabulary was being introduced to the world.

Not only was the technology new to the general public, but it was also new to all of us. We were also trying to understand how to sell the service.

We had to figure out how to explain cellular telephones to people who had been stopping at phone booths to communicate when they were out of the office or away from home. Now we had something new to offer them, a better and faster way to do business.

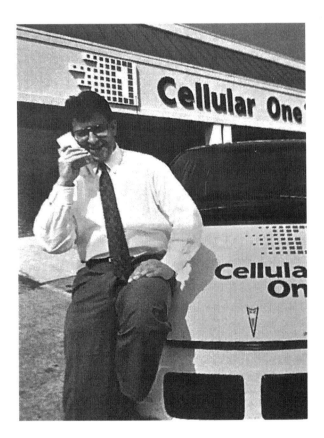

This is me in front of the Cellular One business office in Chattanooga, Tennessee in 1987, talking on what we all referred to back then as the "brick phone."

But it wasn't an easy sell. A call from a phone booth was only twenty-five cents. The average cost of a cellular phone was $1,200. Try selling that to a hard-headed, third-generation, educated country club member or business owner. We charged one-hundred dollars for installation, thirty-five to make the vehicle's horn blow to signal an incoming call, a thirty-five dollar access fee, and thirty-five cents per minute. We were attacking the "If it ain't broke, don't fix it" mindset – and were determined to break it.

Nevertheless, we literally sold the "living daylights" out of cellular phones, and it hasn't slowed down to this day. We destroyed the phone booth business in Chattanooga, and even across the country. Home and office phones with cords, computers and laptops will be the next to go. Anything with a wire connected to it will eventually be toast. We set the pace, giving the world freedom like it had never had before. We changed the way people did business, increasing the volume of work being done in a typical day. Customers even told me they were getting more work done in a day than they had previously accomplished in a week. Imagine that.

Of course, some people resisted the change. Some hard-headed people would say, "I don't want anyone to know where I am." And we would say, "Well, don't tell them." However, the way the world communicated was broken and antiquated, and we fixed it. I was fortunate to be a part of such sweeping change in the U.S. and the world. Hardly a week goes by that I'm not asked something about the continually expanding technology of cellular phones and communications devices. We taught the world what its time was worth, and we had a blast doing it.

For the record, if you make $50,000 per year, you can divide it by 52. It equals $961.53 a week, which divided by 40 hours equals $24.03 per hour. Figure what your time is worth and decide where you want it to be spent. Then go for it!

CHAPTER SEVENTEEN
ACTION STEPS

- Get the picture in your mind of how your family should be living.

- It doesn't matter how long it takes to get there. But the sooner you get started, the sooner you'll get there.

- You don't have to worry about how; just believe.

- Joel Osteen says if you can see the invisible, God can do the impossible.

- See yourself doing the work you enjoy doing.

- See yourself successful and happy with your life.

- See your family doing the things you have never been able to afford until now.

CHAPTER EIGHTEEN

SOME THOUGHTS FOR YOU TO CONSIDER

"To live is the rarest thing in the world.
Most people exist, that is all."
Oscar Wilde

- *When we think bigger, God will show up – and show off.*

- *God expects you to do what you can, and He will do what you cannot.*

- *If you're not uncomfortable sometimes, then you're not challenging yourself enough.*

- *Get out of the safe zone and into the faith zone.*

- *God had the solution before I had the problem.*

- *You can learn more and become worth more than you are now.*

CHAPTER EIGHTEEN

ARE YOU GIVING UP BEFORE YOU EVEN START?

Winners never quit – and quitters never win!

Don't let life put you in a place where you don't want to be. You determine where you'd like to be and set out on a plan to get there. You can make a mountain move – that seemingly unreachable goal or formidable obstacle – if you will believe in your heart that it can.

An old story is told about the Spanish conquistador Hernando Cortés. Whether it's true or not is irrelevant here. The message is clear. When Cortés and his soldiers reached the New World, it is said that the commander ordered his ships burned. With no avenue of escape, the Spanish troops were committed to prevailing in a dangerous and unfamiliar land, or dying in the attempt.

I will never be able to fully express the depth of satisfaction I feel today having made the decision to leave the steel shop and start a new life. It was liberating to find employment in sales, taking a day and planning what I wanted to do – rather than having someone watch everything I did and pay me just enough to stay alive. I had become accustomed to eating a bologna sandwich for lunch, using an upturned five-gallon bucket for a chair. I drive by the old steel shop once a year just to remind myself how it used to be and take a look at the old red truck with no windshield wipers that I drove for twelve years.

I've shaken the dust off my shoes and moved on, but the life lessons of the steel shop will remain with me forever. Once again, I will mention my three perceived "gifts." They worked together to provide me with the determination to become worth more than I was: I was denied food stamps. My plea for a dollar raise was turned down. And I was fired from my first sales job. Reflecting on these experiences, I understand that if they had not happened I would never have found Cellular One. Be ready when the opportunity of a lifetime comes along.

CHAPTER EIGHTEEN
ACTION STEPS

- Don't give yourself a way out.

- It's good to remember where you once were and reflect on it from time to time.

- It's time to move on and kick the dust off your shoes.

- Be ready when your opportunity reveals itself.

CHAPTER NINETEEN

SOME THOUGHTS FOR YOU TO CONSIDER

"Make no little plans; they have no magic to stir men's blood...
Make big plans, aim high in hope and work."
Daniel H. Burnham

- *God will put you in the right place.*

- *God will put His hand in your hand.*

- *Don't leave this Earth with your dreams inside you.*

- *Don't look back on your life wishing you had tried harder.*

- *Behind every great man is a great woman — rolling her eyes!*

CHAPTER NINETEEN

DIRTY AT THE CHAMBER MEETING

"Blasting my past into oblivion."
G.H.

Who or what is the Chamber of Commerce? I didn't even know the organization existed or anything about its purpose. The first meeting of the Chattanooga Area Chamber of Commerce I attended was held at the Chattanooga Convention and Trade Center. When I walked into the luncheon, the tables were set with floral centerpieces that were three feet high. Pineapples had been cut in half, and chicken salad was piled in them.

I looked around to see if there were any other men in the room. I had never been to a meeting like this, and certainly had never attended a luncheon with white tablecloths and pineapples filled with chicken salad. It appeared to be one of those "which fork and which spoon should I use" types of meals. This was just the first of many such luncheon meetings for me. The Chamber meetings became real opportunities to meet people and learn some of the finer points of networking in the business world.

At this first Chamber luncheon, I felt very unsure of myself. You could say I felt like the proverbial fish out of water. But I lived through it, and you can survive uncomfortable "firsts" like this as well. The truth is, when you feel unsure in a room full of people, you can bet some of them are feeling the same way. The good news is it gets easier and easier. Venture outside your comfort zone, take a risk or two, and it will work out just fine.

I've heard it said that if you get nervous in a room full of people, just picture everyone in their underwear and that should take your mind off of you.

From that day on, I went to every luncheon I could attend. Cellular One sponsored or had an employee involved in many of the organizations in town. They included the Jaycees, Big Brothers-Big Sisters, the Heart Association, March of Dimes, the Lung Association, Rotary Club, Kiwanis, Blood Assurance, the Home Builders Association, Associated General Contractors, and the American Diabetes Association. For fifty-eight months I had met an average of 2.8 people per day. Now I was meeting 10 to 100 people per day. You can't add up what the value of meeting people can have on your career.

Our company also advertised on many radio stations in Chattanooga. Cellular One people attended black-tie events all over town. I learned to play golf by playing in the golf tournaments we were sponsoring. We joined the country clubs and private clubs around town. We were corporate sponsors of the annual Riverbend Festival, which has grown into one of the premiere events of its kind in the Southeast. Cellular One was deeply committed to supporting the Chattanooga area. We worked hard at giving back to the community.

Back to that initial Chamber of Commerce meeting: When I walked into the convention center that first time, with a thousand people all dressed up and looking and acting like they owned the place, I started to feel like I didn't belong there. There is always some reason to feel that you are not good enough. We all can have those feelings from time to time.

Where was everybody from our company? And what was I doing in a place like this? I knew the company had reserved a table, but where was it? I found Harry and all the other employees already sitting down. They should have been walking around, meeting people and networking. (At the time, I didn't even know what networking was.)

Everyone else from Cellular One already had a seat, and there was no place for me at the table. I was dusting myself off, and the others were looking at me curiously. I had been to a new, upscale subdivision looking for potential customers and walking around on construction sites. I had mud and dirt all over my shoes, pants and coat, and hadn't noticed it until I got to the table. My Cellular One colleagues laughed at how dirty I was, along with my effort to quickly make myself more presentable.

The issue at hand was finding somewhere to sit, and almost everyone in this spacious hall had already found a table. Once again, thank God, I had read Dale Carnegie's book, *How to Win Friends and Influence People*. Everyone should read this book. It certainly helps in a difficult social situation like this. The Dale Carnegie books include useful information that will help anyone in sales, particularly those applying for sales jobs that need to learn the basic, foundational elements of meeting people.

Today, I try to read one book per month, rotating from books on sales skills to biographies of individuals who have persevered through adversity. The most gut-wrenching book I have read is *Left to Tell* by Immaculee Llibagiza, the true story of the Rwandan holocaust and ninety-one days of hope, prayer, hell and freedom.

We have all met people who exhibit great courage and confidence at all times. Well, that day at the convention center I didn't have a lot of confidence. However, when my fellow employees hadn't saved me a seat, it became a fight or flight situation. I decided my only real choice was to find a seat. Walking around the large gathering and looking for a seat actually did me a lot of good. Eventually, I located a seat and found it within me to introduce myself to the others around the table. It was a more valuable experience than sitting at a table with people that I already knew.

Sometimes it's good to be frightened to the bone by pushing yourself to do something new and different. It keeps you young and sharp. Although the learning process can be difficult, it will be worth it.

Go ahead! Stick your neck out and scare yourself. It's worthwhile to feel the fear and push yourself through it. If you're experienced and you haven't felt the butterflies in your stomach for a while, then get back out there. Do it for your family, for the mom who raised you with no father, or for the dad who worked three jobs to put you through school and never got a break. Do it for your grandmother who raised you, when God only knows where your mother was, or your absentee father.

CHAPTER NINETEEN
ACTION STEPS

- Get ready for some new events in your life.

- I guarantee you'll have some fear. Accept it.

- You'll have some feelings of "I can't do it!" Ignore them.

- You're going to feel uncomfortable, but do it anyway.

- You will persevere.

- It will be gut-wrenching at times, but you'll survive.

- Read a "from hell to high water" book or an "I'll do it or die trying" type of book!

CHAPTER TWENTY

SOME THOUGHTS FOR YOU TO CONSIDER

*"Opportunity is missed by most people because
it is dressed in overalls and looks like work."*
Thomas Edison

- *I'm not going to give up. I will not shut up, let up, or back up until I'm taken up.*

- *In business, everyone is looking for someone they can trust.*

- *Anything is worth doing poorly until you learn to do it well.*

- *To succeed, you have to take a few risks, and I'm willing to take risks by calling on successful people.*

- *Learn how to forgive people. Learn how to forgive yourself. Until you forgive, you're continually looking backward.*

CHAPTER TWENTY

GET READY...AND STAY READY!

"Nobody that ever gave his best regretted it."
George Halas

Are you keeping your head up and your eyes open to the possibilities that await you? In the Bible, God told Gideon to march his men to the water. There the Lord did the unimaginable – He reduced the fighting force from 32,000 men to only 300! But through the selection process, God knew the 300 that remained would be ready – and would stay ready.

In my mind, my career was butter and I was a hot knife. That's how we need to be. I was ready to sell something, and the cellular telephone was God's gift to me. I know that with all my heart. As others would say, the stars definitely lined up for me to be part of something that would forever change the way the world does business.

Cellular telephone communication was new to everyone in the late 1980s. I had seen two magazine ads in the *Robb Report*. One of them was on the inside front cover of the summer 1985 edition. It was a picture of the Empire State Building with signals coming from an antenna reaching out to cars, trucks and people. I believed, "I could sell that!" I saw the second ad later in the year. It depicted a businessman in a white suit sitting at a sidewalk café and talking on his briefcase telephone. "Now that's the way to do business," I thought to myself.

Today, it blows my mind to think that I was a laborer and scrap hauler who heard a tape that had been recorded during an Amway meeting somewhere. I don't even remember who was speaking on the tape, but they said it was a good idea to pick up a copy of the *Robb Report* magazine because it was filled with excellent ideas that might motivate someone to do something. Somehow, I had found my way to the tape, while someone else just happened to record the meeting, and still another person mentioned the *Robb Report*. We must be alert to opportunities as they present themselves to us. I believe that's the key: "Seek and ye shall find."

If you are looking for your life, your place, your dream, your destiny, and you look hard enough and think about it day and night, it will reach out and find you. It will walk in front of you, and your eyes will see it clearly. You will experience a moment of discovery. It will happen for you and your family in a fashion similar to how it did for mine.

Dr. Wayne Dyer says to call the things you want into your life and they will come. A change of feeling, he says, is a change of life.

CHAPTER TWENTY
ACTION STEPS

- Read the *Robb Report* magazine. It will open up your eyes.

- Look into the things you hear and see.

- Be alert.

- Get ready – and stay ready – so you won't have to start getting ready when your opportunity of a lifetime comes along.

CHAPTER TWENTY-ONE

SOME THOUGHTS FOR YOU TO CONSIDER

"Don't expect to find life worth living; make it that way."

- *Everything in life is a choice. You don't have to do anything but eat, breathe, and sleep.*

- *Invest in yourself.*

- *My grandmother told me I would never amount to anything.*

- *There are 6.2 billion people on Earth, 312 million in the United States. And today there are 46 million people living at the poverty level in the United States.*

- *When you own your own business, you will know you have made it when you start getting your work done in a half a day's time: Twelve hours, that is.*

- *I asked a man that owned his own business, how long he worked. He said, "I work 'til the work is done."*

- *I asked a man who owned his own business what he did when he got too tired to work. He said, "I lie down on the floor and take a nap."*

CHAPTER TWENTY-ONE

THE FORCE IS IN YOU, SO
FORCE YOURSELF

"Don't grow old wishing you had tried harder."
G.H.

As you read this next section, I hope you can begin to feel and imagine the relief my family and I felt, knowing our future was looking increasingly bright. At last, the constant anxiety of being very near poverty was fading from our mind. We had something to look forward to, dreams that we knew were on the verge of becoming a reality.

This anticipation itself, this expectation, is an important part of what we call happiness. Living from paycheck to paycheck can become a way of life; and it had for us. When there are no expectations of a better day tomorrow, lives and families can fall apart. Money is one of the main reasons people get divorces and families are destroyed.

It doesn't have to be this way for you. Your life can turn around if you will start to make some important decisions. Take a look at the man in the mirror and make the changes you know you need to make. My first two weeks at Cellular One were coming to an end and I hadn't sold a phone. I just knew they were going to fire me for not selling anything during those first two weeks of my employment. In my mind I was day-to-day; I was afraid they were going to give up on me before I got started.

We had sales quotas at Cellular One, and I had never heard those words before: *sales quotas*. My first quota was to sell six telephones per month; I started working at Cellular One on May 15, 1986. I finally sold three telephones during the last two days of the month; the month was half over when I started. I sold one phone to a businessman and two others to a wrecker company. But selling three phones in two days told me something. That equaled 1.5 phones per day. From then on, I felt like I should sell thirty-plus phones a month.

Wow! It happened: *The laborer had sold something.* Maybe they would give me another month to see if I could do this. The next month, I sold seventeen phones and was named "Salesman of the Month," my first full month on the job. When I sold two phones to one company, we discovered that companies would buy more than one phone. That was a big deal. This was the first time that I had ever been paid for doing my best.

I received two hundred dollars for selling a phone, so for selling seventeen phones I made three-thousand four-hundred dollars. I also had a thousand-dollar a month salary and a hundred-dollar per month gasoline allowance. I could not believe I had made so much money, having been used to picking up maybe an extra thirty dollars here and there selling scrap metal.

When I received my paycheck, I took it to the bank and cashed it. When I got home with the money, I took the one hundred dollar bills and lined them up on our bed. Kimberly and I just stood there and stared at them. Our family's lifestyle was about to change. We had done without for long enough. We often talk about the aspects of our lives we're unhappy with – our jobs, our pay, everything. But until you're so sick and tired of something that it makes you puke, then you may not be as sick of it as you say you are.

Having money was a big change for us as a family. Going out to eat was the first big thing we decided to do as a family. This time, we didn't have to narrow the choice to a place where the kids could eat free. We went to a Mexican restaurant, ordered appetizers for the first time in our entire lives and let the kids order whatever they wanted.

This was the first time we allowed the kids to hold a menu in their own hands. They were all sitting there, looking at the menus. They picked out what they wanted to eat this time. To top it off, we had dessert – fried ice cream – **five** of them, one for everybody. We ate and went home. Wow!

Double wow! Triple wow! When's the last time you let your children look at their own menus?

I had a sense of accomplishment that day. A major percentage of the families in the world know the feeling of pressure when they don't have enough money. They're trying to be happy, but they're ready to pull their hair out. I have known and felt this feeling; I also knew I could do better. So can you.

It was a good day for my family. We got to have a nice meal without worrying, and without my being mad at the world and myself. I had finally broken through to the other side. When the money pressure goes away, it's an indescribable feeling. We had waited twelve years for this day.

I was salesman of the month again in July, selling twenty-three phones with a quota of six for the month. Achieving three-hundred-eighty percent of my sales quota produced another four thousand six hundred dollars, along with the one-thousand dollar monthly salary. Altogether, I had earned approximately ten-thousand dollars in two months, compared to the $1,300 dollars a month I had earned as a laborer.

Things were looking up. God had opened up the success door for me and gave me tremendous favor at the time, although I didn't realize it. I still had a lot to learn about the favor of God in my life – the theological term for it is "grace." Our lives were changing: We were doing things and going places that we had only dreamed of. There's a John Denver song that includes the words, "miner's lady stranger to blue water." We were finally headed to the blue water.

When I look back on that time now, I don't remember thanking God enough for what He did for my family. It's easy to forget God when your life feels like a walk in the park. When I got what I wanted, I turned my back on God and went off on my own. I thought I had the tiger by the tail.

CHAPTER TWENTY-ONE
ACTION STEPS

- Never give up. I wish I could think of something else to say to you to help you see your possibilities.

- Visualize what it's going to feel like when you break free of the chains.

- Think about how your children will benefit from seeing you hang in there, persevering until you succeed.

- Give someone an example to follow.

- When you decide to go for it, the floodgates will open up. What was unclear will become perfectly clear.

CHAPTER TWENTY-TWO

SOME THOUGHTS FOR YOU
TO CONSIDER

*"Insanity is doing the same thing over and over again,
but expecting different results."*

- *Are you using your abilities? If not, then why not? It has been said and proven that the average person uses only seven percent of his God-given talent. It's up to you to use your talent.*

- *Be friendly, no matter what. Be nice, no matter what. Be caring, no matter what. Be understanding, no matter what. Be loving, no matter what. Be a friend, no matter what. Be what it takes, no matter what.*

- *The greatest pleasure you will ever get is when you see the work and the time you have given to your children pay off.*

- *How proud will your dad be of what you've achieved?*

- *How proud will your mom be, now that she can sleep without worrying about you and how you're doing?*

CHAPTER TWENTY-TWO

BEING NAMED SALESMAN OF THE YEAR

O.M.D.B. – Over My Dead Body!
G.H.

I don't want to die wishing I had given life my best shot. I can't stomach the thought of it.

Have you ever tried to twist the lid off a jar? You tried as hard as you could, and then your wife picked up the jar and took the lid right off? You were almost there, you had it – if only you had stayed with it just a bit longer and not let go. We've all let go at one time or another. It feels like nothing is happening, and we give in and say there's no sense in trying.

If you had hung in there just a little while longer, suddenly the dam would have broken, your ship would have come in – whatever term or cliché you want to use. Instead, you gave up and walked away. What you were striving for was almost there, but you missed it. Sometimes, looking back, we realize what we allowed to slip from our grasp – that's when you really feel sick. Opportunity knocked, but we chose not to answer the door.

In September of 1986, Harry announced the salesman of the year would receive a brand new BMW 325i to drive. Bob Lubell, one of the best salesmen I have ever known, asked me to go with him next door to a restaurant a few steps from the office. Bob was the top salesman when I went to work for Cellular One. He told me about the sales contest, and then predicted that when it was over, he and I would probably not be talking to one another.

Well, Bob was right. We went at it and had ourselves a dogfight, fighting it out every thirty days for salesman of the month. I would win one month, and he would win the next. This went on throughout the year. When we got to December, I was ahead in year-to-date sales; far enough ahead that I didn't think Bob could catch me. Wrong – he did. Bob is a smart guy and as I said, a great salesman. By the middle of the month we were dead even, with two weeks to go.

I got the bright idea that Kimberly needed a car phone and I thought this would be the tiebreaker. I drove her car to the service department two days before the end of the month. When I opened the office and walked into the service area, I turned on the lights. I had thought I was the first one to work that morning, but Bob had already brought his wife's car in before I got there. I could not believe it. He had thought of the same thing on the same day. I hadn't told anyone that I was bringing Kimberly's car in to have a phone installed.

There are times in our lives when we allow things to happen and just let events carry themselves to a natural conclusion. However, there are also times when settling for what happens simply is not good enough. I knew I could not live with losing the contest. I had to find a way to win. I prayed about it and believed things would work out.

Toward the end of the month, I had worked every Saturday. I decided to stay home one Saturday. I was in the yard raking leaves when it hit me: I could not let this go. I went inside, cleaned up, drove to the office and started making phone calls. I had tasted defeat when I was a senior in high school, separating my left shoulder in a regional wrestling match. With that, any hope of an undefeated season was gone. The thought of another setback that felt like that was more than I could bear.

On December 31, 1986, everyone else at Cellular One had gone home. Bob and I were still dead even. Unexpectedly, my telephone rang. On the other end was Bill, my insurance agent. I had not previously talked to Bill about a cell phone – I still had a lot to learn about calling people I knew and telling them what I was doing for a living. He said that he had heard I was in some kind of a sales contest and that if he was ever going to get a cell phone today, New Year's Eve, would be a good day to get it.

I said, "Bill, that's exactly right, and we are down to the wire in the contest." Bill gave me his information for the credit check; I told him we had just one problem. The phone had to be installed in his car today. Our service department had closed for the day, so I asked Bill to drive his truck to a radio specialty shop I had set up to handle the overflow work that the Cellular One shop couldn't handle. They installed and activated that phone on New Year's Eve.

This was the winning phone; validation at last that I could sell something, and excel at doing it.

The prize was mine: Salesman of the year, and a new BMW to drive. Think about it: The winner of this contest was the laborer who'd had four interviews and had not been invited back to any of them. The winner was the guy who parked his pickup truck in the parking lot for one last shot at the job of a lifetime! The margin of victory was one telephone over an entire year of sales. One phone could have separated me from the keys to the BMW!

Often, it doesn't take much to make an enormous difference. It does mean, however, that it's necessary to give it all you've got, all the time. The effort will pay off, and then some. Imagine multiplying your *annual income* by more than six times! That's what the personal changes did for my family. But, and it's a *big But,* I had to be irrevocably fed up with my life before I would do something about it!

I went from making a total of $158,000 over twelve years working as a laborer (slightly more than $13,000 a year) to more than $1 million over the next twelve and a half years. Think about the difference a change of income like that would make for your family. Incredible, right? We all have struggles, but being miserable is not worth it; change is the only way to go.

Bob Lubell and I remain great friends to this day, and we talk to each other at least once a month. Bob was the one that showed me the words written in the Bible that changed my life forever. "Have faith in God" (Mark 11:22). He and I talk about that BMW every now and then. Bob has a lot of **WANT TO** in him as well.

The day the keys to the BMW were given to me was a great moment in my life. I will never be able to convey what it felt like. I was the underdog, the person with no commercial sales experience. We had to leave the office, walk into a place of business, and work through all kinds of questions to convince someone to buy a cellular phone. That's what it took to be the winner of the grand prize. But I don't mean the BMW. The BMW was not the prize. The prize was a new life for my family.

In 1988 I received an award in Laguna Beach, California for being one of the eight top salesmen nationally for Cellular One. A bonus of this trip was receiving tickets for Kimberly and me to attend Super Bowl XXII in San Diego, where the Washington Redskins clobbered the Denver Broncos, 42-10.

Whatever you need to do to make positive changes in yourself and in your life, without question it will be worth it. I knew when the keys fell into my hand that all the naysayers were wrong. All the echoes of, "He'll never do it. How could he? He's never sold anything. He hasn't got a chance!" had faded away.

The manager of our service department admitted to me that he once made a bet with another employee that I would not last ninety days with the company. That BMW shut the mouths of everyone who had seen the laborer trying to be somebody and thought it could never happen.

My friend Harry Hudson always says, *"Success happens when you decide."* Do whatever you have to do to crawl out of the hole you are in. Find your *want to* and let it out! When a man does everything he can do, it makes a difference. Use the talents God has given you, whether you have one major talent or a dozen. If you don't use them, then I believe God will transfer the talents to someone who *will* use them.

Using what God gives you also produces what I call a *"multiplier effect."* Something happens when you do all that you can. Unexplainable results unfold, revealing themselves only when maximum energy is applied. Coal does not turn into a diamond until enough pressure from the weight of the world is exerted against it. A jet aircraft uses sixty percent of its fuel just to get off the ground. That means the most difficult part of anything is getting started. So get started!

My daughter, Camellia, recently had a baby boy and it took her maximum effort to bring that baby into the world. Psalm 139:18 reads, "For you created my inmost being; you knit me together in my mother's womb." God created man, the most powerful force in the universe, and He wants you to become all He intended for you to be.

The force inside you has no boundaries, no limits. Only you can set the limits to the amount of energy and drive you apply to finding the God-given destiny for your life. Ask God to give you strength, and He will give it to you. Isaiah 40:31 advises, "But those who hope in the Lord will renew their strength. They will run and not grow weary; they will walk and not be faint."

Chapter Twenty-Two
Action Steps

- Recognize there's a big difference between doing the best you can and doing whatever it takes. Just giving "some effort" may not be enough — you need to be willing to do everything in your power to accomplish your dreams. And then trust God to do the rest.

- Think about a time in your life when you let go of a dream. How does that feel today?

- Don't let it go this time.

- Do all you can — and then some.

- Dig in with all you have — and then some.

- Push yourself all out — and then some.

- Go the extra mile — and then some.

- Ask God to give you the strength you need. And He will.

CHAPTER TWENTY-THREE

SOME THOUGHTS FOR YOU TO CONSIDER

"Do not go where the path may lead, go instead where there is no path and leave a trail."
Ralph Waldo Emerson

- *We all have disadvantages, handicaps, and circumstances to overcome. What are yours? Maybe your disadvantage could be turned into an advantage. If you could overcome your disadvantage, then maybe you could help someone overcome theirs.*
- *You can accomplish things you never dreamed of if you will try.*
- *A great man was asked to tell a national television audience what he had done to become so successful. His reply was three words: "And then some."*
- *Grit. Unyielding courage. What does it mean? It means that I am going to succeed. I am going to call on someone that has more than me. I know they have more than I do, a bigger house, better clothes, a nicer car, and they take better vacations. But not for long!*
- *I have a plan to buy a "getaway car," a convertible for Kimberly and me. It will be the kind of car we can have fun in, driving across the United States with the top down. A vehicle that affords some "just us time." You should never stop having dreams.*

CHAPTER TWENTY-THREE

PROMOTED: FROM SALESPERSON TO SALES MANAGEMENT

*"If we all did the things we are capable of doing,
we would literally astound ourselves."*
Thomas Edison

After eighteen months in corporate sales, I was promoted to East Tennessee Agent Manager for Cellular One. This was my first promotion in the corporate world. I had gone from four unsuccessful preliminary interviews to being salesman of the year, and now I was getting a promotion. God is good.

In July 1989, I was promoted again to sales manager in Chattanooga. Think about this: I had never been in charge of a sales team. I had been one of the captains of our wrestling team in high school and coached several softball teams; however, to say I had management experience was a significant stretch. But I was hungry, eager to advance. I haven't succeeded in everything I've tried, but that's not the point. The point is to try and try again. Take the collective experience of those times in your life when you gave up and use them to push yourself forward. Remember the sick feeling it gave you when the dust settled and you had time to reflect on your failure to persevere and hang in there?

My promotion to sales manager provided an opportunity to see if I could take over a group of sales people that I did not hire, and work with them and be successful. Remember, just because you're a good salesman, that doesn't ensure you'll be a good sales manager. However, I have a theory: If a salesman's customers like him and will do repeat business with him, then by all likelihood he will have the skill set and general knowledge it takes to become a good sales manager.

I have worked with sales managers who have had no sales experience and were put into the management position only because they had a college degree. They really struggled in trying to help the sales representatives with the aspects of their jobs because they hadn't done it themselves. It is impossible to fully understand what you have not experienced. Without this firsthand experience, they just don't get it.

Sales managers with no real sales experience can only see the company's viewpoint. They have no examples from actual life experiences to substantiate or justify the directions they give. A successful sales manager also has to *want to* work with people in order to be successful. The transition from sales to sales management can be difficult, especially if you inherit a team that belonged to someone else. This is almost always the case. The manager who hired the inherited salespeople either quit, got fired, or to use a more politically correct term, "decided to pursue other interests." The most important characteristic of a successful sales manager is the desire to see — and help other people succeed.

The sales team I led included representatives I had worked with before I was promoted to agent manager. They knew who I was as a salesperson, but they had no clear picture of what I would be like as a sales manager. The sales manager who held the position before my promotion had been in management before he entered the cell phone business. Upper management wanted every city to have two sales managers and two sales teams, so I was given a team.

My boss called the other sales manager and me into his office one morning and told the other manager that he was splitting the team in half. Each of us was to have seven sales representatives reporting to us. The other sales manager was not happy with the decision, and in his situation I would not have been happy either, but Cellular One had decided each city would have two sales teams and two sales managers. Early on the representatives were doing okay with my management style, but that quickly changed when I started to push for better results. Complaints began rolling in, both directly to me and to my boss. They said I was pushing too hard. They were putting notes about me under my boss's door.

Soon everything I did was questioned. Much of this was in response to my questioning what some of our sales people were doing with their time. Several of them had previously gotten by, month after month, without hitting their sales quotas. The situation was new to me, and my personality is that of someone who wants everybody to like him. However, I had to insist they do their jobs. Little did I know how difficult this would be to accomplish.

It's a challenging process to put together a successful sales team in any organization. You want everyone to be working toward reaching their quotas, but sometimes it doesn't work out. A new litany of events was about to occur, none of which I had ever experienced in a work environment.

I had to place some of my representatives on probation, and this was new territory for me. After a few months, I had to let some of the team members go, and this was tough. I had not been able to motivate them to do what they needed to do for their own good, and that bothered me. I couldn't understand why anyone would not do their best to succeed. There was, after all, no limit to the commissions they could receive.

When the time came for my first interview with a prospective sales person, I was totally unprepared. I had thought it would be a piece of cake, but instead I did a terrible job. I had no questions prepared to ask the applicant. I didn't have the job requirements written down and ready for discussion. Worst of all, I really didn't know what I was looking for in a new sales person. I struggled through the interview; when it was over I felt as if I had no business in management and should go back to sales.

I felt lost for a while, winging it and hoping I could figure my new management job out before upper management figured out I didn't know what I was doing. For managers, a key component of success is having a system for hiring people. A well-conceived system will assist in choosing the job candidate that is most likely to succeed. A good system includes adequate preparation for the interview, effective questions, a thorough understanding of the available position and its requirements, and a keen eye for spotting competitive, hungry, talented people.

Team sports and team sales share several similarities, particularly when it comes to the "80/20 rule." The adage that 80 percent of the work is done by 20 percent of the people holds true today. Retaining employees is critical for any business, and by the middle of 1991, I was beginning to see a new team come together. I had interviewed, hired and trained my team, and we were ready to go.

By the end of the year, my sales team was *number one in the country*. We finished number one the following year as well. Many of our phones were sold to large corporations and local government, police and fire departments. We had to submit bids on most of the commercial accounts, and had learned how to get the business.

During one stretch of fewer than three months, we sold two thousand cell phones. A large number of teachers had been invited to attend a meeting to describe the features and benefits of our phone service. When I arrived at the office on the day of the meeting, the parking lot was full of cars. Wall to wall, the building was filled with teachers. I carried fifty-dozen doughnuts inside. It was eight a.m., and when Harry saw me walking down the hall he said, "Who in the world are all these people?"

We had never had a meeting like that, and Cellular One had been in business in Chattanooga for seven years. The sales team was on fire!

The first inexpensive transportable phones were called bag phones, and we sold them like there was no tomorrow. We sold so many of them at one time that the service department people had Band-Aids on their fingers from putting the phones together. For the month of December 1992, my team of seven sold one thousand twenty-four phones. Considering that December is typically a month during which most companies are slowing down for the holidays, this feat was even more remarkable.

That monthly total established me as the top GTE sales manager in the United States. It earned me the Winner's Circle prize, an all-expenses-paid trip to Hawaii. I qualified for the Winner's Circle five years in a row and won twenty-two trips during my twelve years at Cellular One/GTE Wireless.

The company took us to Hawaii four times, as well as Puerto Rico, Cancun, Long Boat Key, Sanibel Island and Key West, Florida, Kiawah Island, South Carolina, Bermuda, and a cruise to the Bahamas. We even earned a trip to Super Bowl XXII in San Diego, where the Washington Redskins defeated the Denver Broncos, 42-10. We sat on the twenty-yard line, just nine rows from the field. Chubby Checker stood on top of a black grand piano and did the twist during the halftime show.

168

This photo of our children Brian, Neil and Camellia is one of our favorites, taken at the beach on a vacation trip to Naples, Florida in 1989. The vision of providing opportunities like this for my family drove me to work toward achieving a better life for us all.

169

That Super Bowl was played in 1988. In just eighteen months I had engaged in an incredible journey. I had gone from fumbling in my pocket for enough change to buy a single lemonade to share with my family and applying for food stamps, to sitting only a few yards from some great professional athletes that had the rest of the world watching.

You can accomplish anything if you *WANT TO* badly enough. I didn't care how hard I had to work. I just wanted my dreams to come true.

Prior to my change of career, we rarely went out of town, and when we did, the hotels where we stayed were distinctive with their use of indoor-outdoor carpet. When we went to the Super Bowl, we stayed at the Surf and Sand Resort in Laguna Beach, California. In the lounge, there were mirrors on the ceiling, and at night the lights on the beach shone on the waves, reflecting in those mirrors as they rolled in and out. In Hawaii, we stayed twice at the Grand Wailea Resort and Spa, one of the finest resorts in the world. Quite a contrast to the short trip we had taken.

These are hotels where the rich and famous stay. How did the scrap-hauling, pothole-filling nobody get there? *"WANT TO"!* It was surreal. But also very real.

On one of the trips, Kimberly and I were taking a helicopter ride over the Kilauea volcano. As music came wafting through our headphones, it was overwhelming. I could hardly believe we were in a place I had only dreamed of getting to see. I didn't think about it at the time, but I know now God opened the door of opportunity for me. If He could divide the Red Sea, then letting me sell cellular phones was nothing by comparison.

I'm very proud that *every member* of my sales teams and every sales manager qualified for every single trip that was offered every year I was with Cellular One/GTE. I wanted everyone to experience what I had experienced, and knew if they ever got there once, they would *want to* go back again and again.

If you are reading this book, I can only hope you have some *WANT TO* that needs to be released. I cannot describe the exhilaration I felt, after having been told my entire life that I would never amount to anything.

Hebrews 11:1 states, "Now faith is being sure of what we hope for and certain of what we do not see." The exciting experiences Kimberly and I were now a part of were everything I had ever hoped and dreamed they could be. Your life follows your thoughts. Every day, practice saying something to lift yourself up – and the people around you as well.

CHAPTER TWENTY-THREE
ACTION STEPS

- If you will work hard, good things will happen for you.

- Don't worry about not knowing every detail about your next step.

- Make up your mind to make it come together.

- You're going to make some mistakes.

- When you get your chance, go full steam ahead.

- Don't let the people win who said you couldn't do it. Prove them wrong.

- Have some mustard seed faith (as Jesus described in Matthew 21:21).

- Stop blaming somebody else.

- Don't lie about your situation – to others, or to yourself.

CHAPTER TWENTY-FOUR

Some Thoughts for You to Consider

"You give but little when you give of your possessions.
It is when you give of yourself that you truly give."
Kahlil Gibran

- *If you want to have a great company, hire someone better than you.*

- *Prisoners think and talk about food.*

- *I needed to be pruned like a tree, losing some things that were holding me back.*

- *There is no finish line. There is too much to do. We all start at different places, but while we are breathing we need to be pushing forward. I'm not talking about finishing a particular task. You can mow your grass and it's already growing back before you're finished; so what's this telling us? We are never done. We can rest, but we cannot be finished.*

- *How good can you be? I can be better than I was yesterday.*

- *When you see someone, say, "Hi. How are you?" In a tone that says you care.*

- *There is no end to the good. Doing good never gets old. And you can die when you're done.*

CHAPTER TWENTY-FOUR

HELPING OTHERS DO IT

*"The unselfish effort to bring cheer to others will be
the beginning of a happier life for ourselves."*
Helen Keller

Helping people become more so they will be worth more – what could be better than that? There is an unwritten rule that goes something like this: I got mine; you get yours. The bottom line of life is this: "If it is to be, it is up to me" (William H. Johnson). You have to take charge of your life. As author Jim Rohn said, "Give up the 'blame game.' The world is willing to pay you what you're worth." But the important thing is this: Are you willing to move Heaven and Earth to accomplish your dreams?

You're one of a kind – there's no one exactly like you, and the world is waiting to discover what special talents you have to offer. Aim to go where you're celebrated, not tolerated. Someone once said, "If you see a turtle sitting on a fence post, you know he didn't get there by himself." How true this statement is. There have been times in my life when I thought I could do anything and I didn't need any help from anyone. The truth is, however, we've all had times when we needed a little help. Sometimes, unfortunately, our friends and families are trying to bring us down rather than help us up.

I can't understand how anyone could feel that refusing to help someone out would actually help them? I know it's good to have struggles. If you have not had any difficulties in your life, I personally feel that you may have missed out on some of life's greatest treasures. James 1:1-4 says, "Consider it pure joy my brothers whenever you face trials of many kinds because you know the testing of your faith develops perseverance. Perseverance must finish its work so that you may be mature and complete, not lacking anything. If any of you lacks wisdom, he should ask God, who gives generously to all without finding fault, and it will be given to him."

The super-successful sales representatives I've hired over the years had a lot in common: they had *"Want To."* It has been said the objective is to hire someone that will make it to the top. Then hire a dad who has three children in a private school, whose wife has friends that have everything under the sun and all they talk about are the vacations they have taken to Hawaii and what color their next Mercedes or BMW will be. This is the kind of guy who will knock himself out to get it done.

It's the hiring manager's job to do everything he can to see that those who report to him are successful. This does not apply only to salespeople, but to any new employee. Training should be a priority for new hires. The management of a company must do everything it can to teach a new employee in detail what is expected of them. They must know how they're supposed to do their jobs, and how their results will be measured.

A vast number of companies fail to train new employees adequately. They let the employee figure out things for themselves – or even worse, they let one of the "eighty-percenters" teach them. This is one of the major reasons that ninety-five percent of all new businesses fail. New hires routinely do not make it through their first year on the job. Hiring the wrong people and not providing proper training are two of the most costly and usually unmeasured errors in any business.

Imagine the cost. If the owners and managers of new businesses would take the time to match job requirements and appropriate training to every position, the failure rate would decrease exponentially. My longtime friend Bill Spencer, a graduate of the United States Military Academy and a retired colonel in the U.S. Army, used to say, "Keep them tight in the beginning."

Bill explained to me that new recruits coming into the Army have to be taught the Army way because their own way of doing things is no longer acceptable. Why is this necessary? The Army has perfected its methodology and its way of doing things. Through the years, the leadership of the Army has determined what works and what doesn't work – and what doesn't work can get people killed.

Bill said a tight rein must be maintained over the recruits at first, with no deviations. This ensures that recruits, or employees for that matter, understand the expectations and the severity of the consequences if there are deviations from the rules. According to Bill, no slack is given until recruits learn the Army way.

I was serving on the local board of directors of the March of Dimes in 1990 when this photo was taken at a major fund-raising banquet. Kimberly and I joined our guests, actor Gary Collins and his wife, Mary Ann Mobley, a former Miss America, and Lewis Smith (in background), a Hollywood actor raised in Tiftonia, Georgia near Chattanooga.

The same should be true for companies. Everyone should have to get results. If you're a manager, keep the employees tight. They will thank you for it later, and so will your company.

How can one person help others to help themselves? It all starts with the correct hire. Find the individual with the skills that fit the job. Sending

175

a duck to "eagle school" will never get results. Even with the hat and the badge that proclaims he's an eagle, the truth will eventually surface. When the duck meets a rabbit, he'll make him his friend rather than prey, not having it within him to do what the eagle would do. It's not in his DNA.

Hiring the right person will take care of ninety-five percent of the failure issues. The rest becomes details, and the right individual will do whatever it takes to succeed. To say helping people find their own way is difficult is an understatement, like saying the Grand Canyon is big. It can be hard, demanding work. But helping a person make small, daily, weekly, monthly and yearly changes will have a longer-lasting effect than pushing for rapid change. Helping someone make life changes will help you become a better you. There is an important reality to keep in mind: Trying to help someone to change is pointless unless they feel the pressure to change themselves. This pressure should come from within. The individual must be motivated to change. Otherwise, the result most often will be failure, debilitating failure that will usually set a person back further developmentally than they had been originally.

Coaching employees becomes quite personal at times. It involves asking them to stop doing something they have done habitually for most of their adult lives. Now you're asking them to think about what they have been doing and to start doing it differently. This will not be natural and it's uncomfortable for any creature of habit to change their behavior. While this will not seem like fun to them, the results will be life-changing.

Seeing positive results and the beneficial effects on an employee's or friend's life makes the effort worthwhile. When change occurs, it affects not only the individual, but also the people and family members around them.

When I walk into a business dressed in a suit and tie, the employees see me as a salesman but never as the laborer, pothole fixer and scrap hauler I once was. There is something else they don't see, particularly if I'm entering a company where physical labor is being done. I can see the wheels turning in their heads and jumping to the conclusion this guy has never had his hands dirty. They can't see any of my struggles, and I can't see any of theirs.

We draw our opinions from the appearances we see. I believe there's a major difference between how we perceive things and how God perceives them. It says in 1 Samuel 16:7, "man looks at the outward appearance, but the Lord looks at the heart."

People often see what they choose to see – good, bad, ugly or indifferent. Fair or unfair, that's the way it goes. I hope this provides you with some ideas about helping the people that are important to you. Encourage them to visualize the benefit of seeing themselves in a different light, the light of their dreams.

I'm glad when I can say to someone, "I know how you feel, but you can do it. You can become the person God intended you to be."

If you hire the right people, the talents are there, waiting to emerge. Helping people to be the best they can be requires a skill set in itself, including a great deal of discipline for the individual who is trying to coach someone to new heights.

The world is populated with talented people who will never have the opportunity to use a fraction of their capabilities. However, there are many ways to motivate people. Fear is a motivator, but I've never used fear. I have no fear of firing someone once I have exhausted my efforts to get results. My best results have come from rewards, encouragement and recognition to motivate people to do their best. I want to spend the rest of my life helping as many people as I can to become the best they can be.

For more than twenty-five years I have been writing down my goals on an annual basis. I take several hours on the first day of January and plan my next year of personal and business goals. I have no doubt that writing down my goals has changed my life. I like what the Bible says in Habakkuk 2:2-3: "Then the Lord replied, "Write down the revelation and make it plain on tablets so that a herald may run with it. For the revelation awaits an appointed time; it speaks of the end and will not prove false. Though it lingers, wait for it, it will certainly come and will not delay."

I've shared this practice with anyone that's interested in hearing about it, and I know it's changed some lives. It will change your life, too, the moment you write down your own goals. Writing them down transforms them from dreams to tangible reality, legitimate targets to aim for over the next year. Having them in writing serves as a reminder to not forget what you're shooting for. And if you want, you can share them with someone else who can hold you accountable and check to see how you're progressing.

I want to tell as many people as I can, "You can do it!" If you *"WANT TO."*

CHAPTER TWENTY-FOUR
ACTION STEPS

- You cannot do it alone, even if you're the best there is.

- There will be some trials and setbacks. You just have to pick yourself up and go again.

- Look for the twenty-percent people, not the eighty-percent people.

- If you help people get what they want, you will get what you want.

- Some days you will feel like you are in over your head. Keep going.

CHAPTER TWENTY-FIVE

SOME THOUGHTS FOR YOU TO CONSIDER

"You have not lived until you have done something for someone who can never repay you."

- An elder in Sunday school said that he sometimes starts a fight with his wife just to make up with her.

- What bothers you the most? Is it not having what you want, or is it having someone tell you, "No"?

- To have a great harvest, you have to sow a lot of seeds.

- Money will not make you happy. Being generous will make you happy.

CHAPTER TWENTY-FIVE

'HAVE TO' VERSUS 'WANT TO'

"Without ambition one starts nothing.
Without work one finishes nothing.
The prize will not be sent to you. You have to win it."
Ralph Waldo Emerson

It's a simple fact that sooner or later, we all will have a rainy day. Maybe more than one. The rain comes in many forms. You become too sick to work. Your job changes in ways you weren't expecting. You get fired; or unexpected expenses occur. The list could go on and on. We've all got personal and business issues, many of them not easy to solve. But as Jim Rohn says, "start doing different things with what happens to you; and give up the blame game."

The sun will come up tomorrow and a new opportunity will be waiting. But when your life is on fire and you don't have a water hose, it's tough. That's why it's so important for you to be working on you. I want to make this perfectly clear: Working on making yourself more valuable. In other words, to have more you need to become worth more. You can become worth more tomorrow if you will work on you today.

When you're in a *have-to* situation it doesn't take much to be motivated. You don't have a choice. Your goal is to separate your abilities from your disabilities. And then, focus all your energy on your strongest abilities and capitalize on them. The right coaching can take a person who has been told or feels like they have been dealt a losing hand and turn the situation into a winning hand.

Start looking around at the people you come in contact with and begin to ask them some questions. Ask about their families and then move on to what they do for a living. After you have shocked everyone you know by asking them questions, you can move on to the people that will help you. It's not going to kill you to ask someone a question. Besides, after you ask the question, all you need to do is nod your head. They'll do all the talking.

By doing this, you can start to build a network of people that you can call on for advice and expertise. They sometimes call these groups of advisor associates, "Master Mind" groups. Remember, the only place where success comes before work is in the dictionary. Why don't we make changes before we're in a crisis? The fact is most people have never been taught how to work. The sooner you get started, the sooner you will begin to move closer to the person you want to be.

I never wanted things to be easy. I only wanted them to be possible. Don't wish *things* were easier – wish *you* were better. Remember the wisdom of Jeremiah 29:11, which offers this promise: " 'For I know the plans I have for you,' " declares the Lord, " 'plans to prosper you and not harm you, to give you hope and a future.' " God has provided an ocean of opportunity just waiting for you to jump in.

CHAPTER TWENTY-FIVE
ACTION STEPS

- Why are you waiting until it's almost too late to get started?

- Today is the best day to start making your moves.

- Tomorrow will never come. As someone has said, "Today is the tomorrow you worried about yesterday."

- Find some people who will give you some honest opinions on what you need to do.

- Make a punch list of the areas you need to work on.

- Make a list of your best skills and polish them until they turn into diamonds.

- Remember you are going to have many great days ahead.

CHAPTER TWENTY-SIX

SOME THOUGHTS FOR YOU TO CONSIDER

"The world is before you, and you need not take it or leave it as it was when you came in...."
James Baldwin

- *Only the things God has made are as good as they can be in every way. Could I produce a better sunrise or sunset? Who could love more than God loves us? But for things within our grasp, we can always strive for improvement. So, let's get started. We have a lot of work to do, and time is running out. Buckle up. We've got to get out of this place!*

- *You don't have to be successful at everything to be successful in life. You only need to be successful at a few things — the things you do each day. Not only does it affect you, but it also affects the people around you.*

- *I need to see people as they can be, not as they are.*

- *We need to pray more about things before we go into them, rather than waiting until we encounter difficulties to pray.*

- *I hear and I forget. I see and I remember. I do and I learn.*

CHAPTER TWENTY-SIX

GOING FOR IT AGAIN – LEAVING THE JOB THAT CHANGED MY LIFE

"Cut out all the ropes and let me fall."
Bon Iver's song

In February 1998, I resigned from GTE. Working for Cellular One and GTE had changed my life. My years working with both companies had given me the opportunity to experience things I had only imagined, and that confirmed my belief that if you try – and try again – you can succeed in this life. My last job with them was serving as manager of the GTE retail stores in Cleveland, Tennessee.

I decided to go to work for a new wireless company that had been awarded a cellular license in Chattanooga, one of the first cities in the United States to have a third wireless carrier. Prior to that time, major U.S. cities had only two carriers, one landline and one wire line. Chattanooga's cellular carriers before then had been BellSouth and GTE Wireless. This was a major change in the wireless industry across the United States. Competition increased dramatically as the number quickly grew over the next couple of years to as many as six cellular companies in every city.

When I resigned from GTE, which is now Verizon Wireless, I had two of the top retail stores in America. The reason for the success was our team members. From my assistant Shelia to the administrative staff and the sales team, they were as good as it gets. Many of them are still there today. I left because I was bored with doing only retail. Previously, I had been in charge of the entire operation. GTE had decided to change the management of its three sales distribution channels: retail stores, major accounts, and agents. Rather than having one manager over all three areas, the idea was to have a different manager over each.

I had hired every employee in the area, and I didn't like the change. GTE's decision was the right one, but I was looking for a bigger challenge. I had no idea that within fourteen months I would be standing in the unemployment office wondering what had happened. But we have already talked about, things happen for a reason. My new job responsibilities included developing the marketing and sales plans for a new carrier in Chattanooga. I hired all the managers of the sales staff and built a business plan with projections and compensation for all the sales people and managers.

One year after starting the business from scratch, however, the owner sold the company. It had been a year of new experiences for me. Months earlier, we had made a trip to New York City to meet with venture capitalists to raise money to start the business. I still have the two boxes of matches I picked up when I walked across the street from our hotel to the World Trade Center. Those buildings, of course, are now destroyed after the September 11, 2001 World Trade Center attacks.

I remember going to the top floor of one of the towers and standing in the restaurant to see what New York looked like from such a height. The view was incredible. *As you pursue your own dreams, letting loose of your past limitations, your view will be as well!*

Chapter Twenty-Six
Action Steps

- My decisions in life have been made from my gut. This might not work for you. It will take some getting used to.

- When it doesn't work out the way you hoped, it's not the end of the world.

- Remember that when one door shuts, anticipate that another one is about to open – and it will be better than the last.

CHAPTER TWENTY-SEVEN

SOME THOUGHTS FOR YOU TO CONSIDER

"Unrest of spirit is a mark of life; one problem after another presents itself and in the solving of them we can find our greatest pleasure."
Kal Menninger

- *Abraham Lincoln said, "I don't like that man. I need to get to know him better."*

- *Once there was a great chess player who visited many of the famous museums of Europe to relax and gather his thoughts. He happened upon a painting of the Devil playing chess with a young man. The game appeared to have reached checkmate. The great player asked for a chessboard. Placing the board in front of the painting, he placed the pieces on the board in identical positions. A smile came to his face when he discovered the young man had one more move available. God will give you one more move, too.*

- *When you say, "Good morning!" to someone and they just say, "Fine," back to you, maybe you should say, "Fish guts!" and see if they still say, "Fine."*

- *When you hunger enough for your needs, then maybe you'll be willing to take the actions necessary to fulfill them.*

CHAPTER TWENTY-SEVEN

I WANTED TO START A BUSINESS OF MY OWN

"There are but a few times in this life when you feel total elation; enjoy them."
G.H.

I could not let the dream go – I had to start my own business. The goal of owning a business had been with me for a long time. I didn't know how it would turn out, but I had to try. Trying was more important to me than the end result, and I couldn't postpone this desire any longer. I have a friend, Adrien, who often says, "Don't be a tomorrow man, because tomorrow never comes. You're in your tomorrow right now." And he's right.

My life was about to change once more. A new chapter was beginning, one that would test everything about me and drastically redefine my world as I knew it. For twenty-five years, I had carried in my wallet a card with my goals written on it. Over the preceding ten years, one of the written goals had said, "Own your own business." I had written down that same goal for an entire decade! None of my other goals had been written down this many times. I had been writing goals for twenty-five years, accomplishing them and changing them, but had never written down a goal for so long without accomplishing it or changing it. This was different.

My push, or better yet, my opportunity, came when I lost my job because our company was sold and the new owners wanted to bring in their own people to implement the new strategic plan. I had been successful at selling cellular phones, motivating people and building out cellular territories, but had not yet identified the business I wanted to start.

GTE had rewarded me for doing well. For twelve years I'd been recognized as one of the best of the best. It made me nauseous to think about being anything less than number one. Today, I believe the feeling that has pushed me to succeed is predominantly related to fear – fear of failing. All of my life I've had to prove myself. At Cellular One it was no different. Before going there, I had no experience in sales and no record of success to back me up.

As a young man, this gold office building in Chattanooga, Tenn., once known as "the Blue Cross building," always intrigued me. Years later, our Cellular One team was able to sell a lot of cellular phones there.

I suppose I've kept myself on permanent probation, starting the day Harry put me on formal probation when he hired me. Selling fewer phones in one month than I had the previous month was reason enough for my internal alarm to go off. Now, it was gut-check time: Did I really want to own my own business and run the show? The answer was an undeniable, "Yes!"

On the Friday night after I lost my job, Kimberly and I drove downtown to see a movie. On the way, we were trying to think of a name for the business. I was joking with her, saying I wanted to name it Big Gary's Wireless Store, Wireless World, or Planet Wireless.

I said to Kimberly, "Well, we want everybody to talk wirelessly." Then, we said to one another, "Talk Wireless!" A name was born: The business was officially named Talk Wireless, Inc., or TWI.

The following Monday, I went to the Hamilton County Courthouse and bought my first business license. We opened our first retail store in July 1999. By 2004, we had opened thirty retail stores in Tennessee, Georgia, South Carolina, and Kentucky. We were one of the top ten retail agents in the country for sales volume, selling over a thousand phones some months. That was significant production from an independent sales agent in the wireless industry.

The part of the business that will always mean the most to me was the opportunity to work with Kimberly and seeing how talented she is in every aspect of running a business. In addition to working with her, I brought my sons, Neil and Brian, and my daughter, Camellia, on board. All five of us worked together opening stores.

We spent a lot of time together, riding to our stores and looking for new locations. These times gave me the opportunity to talk with the kids for hours. I regard these as some of the best years of my life. As a family and a team, we all worked exceptionally hard to be successful.

In 2006, when I had had all the retail business I could stand, we sold TWI. I was ready to move toward the next chapter of my life. We had begun building a business in 1999, and within forty-eight months it was producing $3.7 million in annual revenue.

I know my children will always remember the time we had together and what they learned about running a business – how to hire people, how to interview and train them, and most important, how much they learned about themselves. These lessons will stay with them the rest of their lives, and I thank God I had the opportunity to work with all of them.

Chapter Twenty-Seven
Action Steps

- Understand that owning your own business is not for everyone.

- I would not have been happy if I had not started my own business.

- The main reasons most businesses fail are 1) a lack of experience, and 2) a lack of sufficient cash/capital, and 3) location, location, location.

- If you are going to start a business you need a team. The team consists of an attorney, banker, a CPA – and God. (And not necessarily in that order!)

CHAPTER TWENTY-EIGHT

SOME THOUGHTS FOR YOU TO CONSIDER

"Life is like a game of cards. The hand that is dealt you represents determinism; the way you play it is free will."
Jawaharlal Nehru

- *Things to quit doing: 1) Waiting on next week — it may never come. 2) Procrastinating — just get on with it. 3) Trying to get everything just right — it's never, ever going to be just right.*

- *It didn't happen to me. It happened **for** me.*

- *Even Jesus fell under the weight of the cross, but Simon carried it for Him. God sent Simon to help Him carry the load.*

- *Oh-No Zone: Oh no, they might not like me. Oh no, my teeth are crooked. Oh no, I'm tall. Oh no, I'm short. Oh no, I'm smart. Oh no, I'm dumb. Oh no, I'm skinny. Oh no, I'm fat. Oh no, I'm uneducated.*

- *Grace is receiving what I need instead of what I want.*

CHAPTER TWENTY-EIGHT

'YOU HAVE NO EXPERIENCE'

"Ability will never catch up to the demand for it."
Confucius

Banking? Are you crazy? You cannot even spell "bank." Yes, today I am a banker. When I started yet another career, I had no banking experience, no finance degree. In fact, even after I had been in the field for about six months, a senior commercial banker insisted that customers would never bank with me because I had no experience.

I believe God gives some people struggles so they can use the experiences to help others. A few years ago, I felt God was punishing me for something I had done. I know differently now. Difficult times can strengthen us and prepare us for even greater things.

Some time ago I came across a quotation from Confucius that addresses this: "Our greatest glory is not in never failing, but in rising every time we fall." A friend also has a wall plaque that states, "Life isn't about waiting for the storm to pass…it's about learning to dance in the rain."

After Kimberly and I sold TWI, it was time to find a new career. I updated my résumé (a real one this time) and started making phone calls. I was looking for something to do with the rest of my life. I prayed for two things: I asked God to put me in a position where I could just be myself, and for a place where I could help people. I didn't care what the position was.

Someone told me that banks were changing the way they did business, meaning that they were hiring sales people who would actually go out and call on companies. I was told I should look into banking. Well, I did. I started talking to everyone I knew who worked at a bank. I wish I could remember the person who told me to take the chance. Whoever it was, I believe God told them to say what they said. I thank them and ask God to bless them and their family.

This effort did not result in a single interview. When you are in need of help, it sometimes seems your friends avoid you and would rather do anything than assist in opening up a door for you. I asked everyone I knew about their bank and who they knew who might help me to at least gain consideration for employment. Nothing happened.

I had three people that I had known for twenty years tell me I would not last a single month as a banker. As soon as the customers figured out I was not born a banker, and especially since I didn't have a degree in banking, I would never succeed in banking. They had a really big laugh just talking about it.

Well, it did happen. I got a phone call from Rita Prince, a friend from the wireless business. She asked if I would allow her to use my name as a reference on a job application.

"No problem, Rita," I replied. "Tell whoever you are talking to that they can give me a call. I'd be glad to help you."

Then Rita asked what I had been doing since I had sold my business. I told her I was trying to get a job as a commercial banker and driving downtown for an interview at that very moment. She told me when I finished my interview I should take my résumé to her husband, Dick Prince, my former sales trainer at GTE. Dick had changed careers himself, taking a job with a bank. Rita said Dick would take care of getting me an interview with his bank – and he did.

In Mark 11:22-24, Jesus tells us, "Have faith in God. I tell you the truth, if anyone says to this mountain, 'Go, throw yourself into the sea,' and believes in his heart that it will happen, it will be done for him."

After five interviews, I was hired on November 20, 2006. I've been one of our bank's ten lenders for more than six and a half years. How is it possible to break into a new career like banking with no experience, no banking degree, and an economy in its worst condition in more than thirty years?

I believe when you make up your mind to do something that's going to determine your livelihood, things will start to happen. Your energy, personal resolve, motivation and all-out effort will rise to a level that's seldom seen in normal, everyday circumstances. When failure isn't an option, amazing things do happen. Banking has proved to be a rewarding experience for me.

From the start, I had confidence that it might work out, but my hopes had been dashed temporarily by three not-so-good friends that had given me only words of discouragement. I felt like I had a 50-50 chance to make it in banking. If you believe and put forth the effort, something good will happen. By the way, I did erase the phone numbers of those three individuals from my cell phone. I didn't want to see their names show up on my caller ID ever again.

Working at the bank has given me the opportunity to get my feet underneath me again. I've been able to spend some real quality time thinking about what I want to do with the rest of my life. God has made this latest chapter of my life a good one. The perception is that banking is difficult and complicated. Even though the banking industry is in disarray at this time and banks are closing all over the country, one thing is always true: If you're a giver and not a taker, some mind-boggling changes will happen.

God opens doors when we work toward our divine destiny with only faith to sustain our forward motion. So much for no degree, no experience, no portfolio, and those that said, "There is no way he can make it in banking."

Before Mom passed away, I took her to see a billboard with my picture on it that advertised our bank. When we drove up to the billboard, my photo was there, and Mom could not believe what she was seeing. She cried and cried. I could only imagine what was going through her mind. She didn't have to say anything. Actually, she couldn't talk for five minutes. She asked me if she could have the picture when they took it down. It was thirty-feet by fifteen-feet. Only someone's mom would ask a question like that.

My wife, Kimberly, has wisely observed, *"We can't all sell, but we all buy. So, if you can sell, you are in a select group."*

Holding these portraits of my biological father, James E. Aslinger, and my mother, Sara Stone, is literally the only way I have ever seen them together.

CHAPTER TWENTY-EIGHT
ACTION STEPS

- You can do something different – you really can.

- The life skills you have will serve you well in a completely new adventure.

- Take a shot at a new way to make a living. Do what you *want to* do, not what you *have to* do.

- Do some networking and something good will catch your eye.

- If you will take action, the doors will begin to open up for you.

- A new opportunity will materialize just for you.

- Believe in your abilities. If you were good once before, you will be as good or better the second time, or the third, or the fourth or...you get the picture.

CHAPTER TWENTY-NINE

SOME THOUGHTS FOR YOU TO CONSIDER

"Go out into the world where your heart calls you. The blessings will come, I promise you that. I wish for you the insight to recognize the blessings as such, and sometimes it's hard. But you'll know it's a blessing if you are enriched and transformed by the experience. So be ready, there are great souls and teachers everywhere. It's your job to recognize them."
Sy Montgomery

- *A man who spent a lot of time on the road decided to write his wife a letter every day. She fell in love with the postman. Moral of the story: Don't stay away too long from what's important to you.*
- *Do not get the loser's limp. When a football player cannot catch the runner, he sometimes gets up from the ground with a limp. Don't make excuses.*
- *We cannot comprehend the consequences and limits of relying upon ourselves alone.*
- *It takes an irritation inside the oyster to make a pearl. How irritated are your insides? Is a "pearl" forming in you?*
- *"I got here as quick as I could!"*

CHAPTER TWENTY-NINE

I CAN FIX IT MYSELF

"Life is hard without God."

"Life's tragedy is that we get old too soon and wise too late." This clever observation by Benjamin Franklin describes me. It took me half of my life to learn that God is the answer to every aspect of living. I thought that handling my problems and issues by myself was what it meant to be a man. I can't begin to imagine how much farther along in life I would have been – and how much quicker I would have gotten there – if I'd had the wisdom to ask *God for wisdom*. What I've learned since is that if you ask, He'll be glad to give it to you.

Believing I can fix any problem myself has caused me considerable anguish at times. Diving headlong into a problem or new opportunity has never been difficult for me. I've always been able to decide where I want to go, take off in that direction and figure out the steps necessary to be successful as I went along. Does that sound familiar to you?

Kimberly and I had been in our own cellular phone business for about four years when the situation began to create stress in our lives in ways that we had never experienced. Until that time, we had been a debt-free business. We were opening stores, and everything was paid for in a couple of months. All that began to change in November 2004, and the experience was transforming.

That November, we changed our method of operation from selling phones and collecting two hundred dollars at the point of sale to selling phones and not collecting any money. Our carrier had made a decision to initiate a promotional campaign at the beginning of the holiday season. We were not obligated to participate in the promotion, but if we had not participated when all our competitors did, we would have been dead in the water.

This promotion drastically impacted our cash flow. We had been selling hundreds of phones each month at a cost of two hundred dollars per unit, so when the promotion began and the bills started to come in, we didn't have the money to pay them. Our account was supposed to be credited for the sales, but this didn't happen as it was supposed to, and when we did get the credit it was never for the correct amount. We hired an employee to work exclusively on this problem, since it became a constant battle to get paid every month.

The timing of everything was completely out of whack. The cash flow was not sufficient to meet the demands of payroll and rent, or any other fixed costs associated with operating the business. Trying to smooth out the peaks and valleys, I secured lines of credit with three different banks, including a home equity line of credit on my personal residence. All the credit totaled seven hundred thousand dollars, and it still wasn't enough.

There was no way to make up the cash deficiency. Something had to give. By the middle of 2006, we were at the end of our rope. We could not resolve the issues with our carrier, and I had reached my breaking point. I couldn't understand why we couldn't get paid correctly each month. Everything was based on the activation of phone numbers, and the carrier assigned the numbers. All the phones came from the carrier, so what was the problem?

We had backup documentation, but it was never good enough. The carrier's area sales manager suggested we install a point of sale system to track each sale. We did. Nothing improved.

One day the pressure of keeping the business together was so intense I was beginning to shut down physically and emotionally. I experienced severe chest pain and was concerned something was going to happen to me physically. I didn't want to die at the office in front of my children, so I walked around and made small talk with everyone. Then I told them I would be back in a few minutes. I went home and lay down on the sofa to die. It sounds crazy, but that's what I did. I should have gone to the hospital, but didn't want to.

After lying there for a while, guess what? You guessed right – I did not die. Suddenly, I started to feel better, and the pain was gone. For a time, I sat on the sofa and thought about being alive. What was I going to do with the rest of my life? God had put my nose against the floor, and I asked him to forgive me. I had to put Him in charge of my life.

This was only the second time I had asked God to help me. For years, I had listened to people at church pray for help. Well, not me! I was going to be a man. I was not going to ask God to help me with anything I could do myself.

Somewhat reluctantly, I decided to ask the elders of our church to meet with me. I knew I needed to talk to someone about what was going on in my life. In the meeting, one of the elders that I thought highly of asked me a question. He said, "Gary, are you praying about this?" My answer became a defining moment.

I replied, "No, no. I'm not." He looked at me in disbelief and said, "Well, how's that going for you?" The answer was readily apparent: "Not too good!" It wasn't going well at all.

That was the last day I haven't asked God to guide me in everything that I do. Proverbs 2:6 says, "For the Lord gives wisdom, and from his mouth comes knowledge and understanding." Then Psalm 102:17 says, "He will respond to the prayer of the destitute; he will not despise their plea." Shortly after that day, God made the impossible possible – we sold the business. We were free. Thank God Almighty, we were free!

I believe in my heart that God has a plan for all of us, and the writing of this book is going to lead me to the next chapters in my own life.

I've spent countless hours visualizing how I can give my family the life I've always wanted them to have. Some visions I keep to myself. Others I've shared with Kimberly. I believe the rest of my life is going to be the best of my life!

CHAPTER TWENTY-NINE
ACTION STEPS

- It's hard to comprehend why our lives come unraveled at times. I felt as if God was punishing me for something I had done. He wasn't punishing me – He was preparing me for the next chapter of my life.

- I now know there are many seasons to a lifetime. And I have learned to appreciate all of them.

- Worrying will not do you any good. If the birds do not worry, why should you?

- Being a man does not mean you don't ask God to help you. It means knowing you are no good without Him.

- Don't do what I did and have to learn that the hard way.

CHAPTER THIRTY

SOME THOUGHTS FOR YOU TO CONSIDER

"Wheresoever you go, go with all your heart."
Confucius

- The term *"sales area"* defines the area where an ordinary person can achieve extraordinary results with effort.

- It took 100 years to put a cap on the bottom of a ketchup bottle. What was research and development doing all that time?

- My wife prays for me. She says, "Lord, help us!"

- When trouble comes, lean on God. Even when you don't have any trouble, lean on God.

- My son, Neil, says pain is just fear leaving your body.

- Dream, dream, dream on until your dreams come true.

CHAPTER THIRTY

IMPORTANCE OF THE RIGHT MINDSET

"He who is not courageous enough to take risks
will accomplish nothing in life."
Muhammad Ali

The mind is a very powerful force in our lives. Experts say we only use a small fraction of our brain capacity. So why is it that we're satisfied with this minimal amount of effort? How can we leave such a vast amount of power untapped?

I believe the main reason we aren't using our brainpower is the lack of *belief*. How can I say this? For one reason, I have experienced the power of believing in my own life. When I have written goals down and then seen them materialize, I know it wasn't luck. Luck didn't have anything to do with it. The goals were specific to me, so when something came about, bam there it was. It was the power of believing – and if you don't believe me, try it. Try believing with all your heart and see what happens. If you will believe for just a short period of time, it can and will produce results.

I'm not suggesting you go too far out on a limb at first. But with practice you can work up to some real life-changing believing. Remember, it only takes a mustard seed amount of belief to have an impact on everything around you.

What about accomplishing things? Accomplishment on its own isn't enough — it's the pursuit and the satisfaction of knowing you've given it everything you've got. It's not good grammar, but I like the statement I heard some time ago: *"Having everything ain't nothing, unless you're happy."* And part of being happy is knowing you've done all you could, you were willing to take a risk, and as they say in sports, you left it all on the field.

I believe that when you make up your mind to do something, you immediately become closer to whatever it is you want to achieve. I know from my own experience that this is true.

In 1954, Roger Bannister *made up his mind* to break the four-minute mile. That barrier had stood for centuries. Before Bannister decided to do whatever it took to shatter the mythical barrier, the world had decided a man could not run fast enough and long enough to complete a mile run in less than four minutes. But Bannister ran a mile in 3:59.4, and it didn't kill him.

By 1999, the four-minute mark had been broken nineteen times. By 1999, a total of 16.27 seconds had been shaved from the four-minute benchmark. It took forty-five years for that much time to be cut. Why did it take so long?

I can only speculate that we accomplish things in small, incremental steps. Maybe this is God's way of keeping us humble. Too much success at one time may hurt us more than help us. I think the amount of belief we have in ourselves works hand in hand with the amount of success we achieve. The pace of improvement is connected to the belief and the mindset we cultivate within our minds.

Yes, we do see images of success in our mind's eye. But these images are continually changing. One minute we see fantastic accomplishments for ourselves and our families. The next minute, we see the work necessary to achieve the goals and the images of success start to lose their luster. We settle for less and less as the days pass, and allow our dreams to fade away. We start to justify not taking action by saying things like, "I have it better than my mom and dad had it. I'm not doing so badly."

You have what it takes; you can break the family chains. You can achieve more than anyone in your family has ever achieved or dreamed of achieving; you're about to go where no one in your family has ever gone.

Make the changes you need to make. If you don't know what you need to do to improve yourself, then ask someone who has what you want how they were able to achieve success. But be prepared. It may feel crazy to let someone know that you want what they have, but believe me – they'll love to tell you about it.

If your bank account needs a transfusion and you haven't eaten out with your family in a year or two, then wake up and realize no one is going to fix your problem. You must change your thoughts from despair to hope, to belief, to expectation, and finally, to receiving and believing.

Second Corinthians 1:10 says, "He has delivered us from such a deadly peril, and He will deliver us. On Him we have set our hopes that He will continue to deliver us."

It doesn't matter how big your mountain is. It doesn't matter how washed up and low down you happen to feel. You can claw your way back to life. It will be better the next time around, and you can always show the claw marks to your new friends.

Start the process of believing in yourself. It will help to remember some of your prior successes, large and small. Make a list of your successes – anything and everything you feel good about.

I understand the voice, the sick feeling that says to you, "I'm no good for anything anymore." I believe this sinking feeling will try to bring you to the lowest point it can before it kills you. The only difference is you're still alive and breathing. If you can still fog a mirror when you breathe on it, then God has something He needs you to do. The dream is still there, and it always will be there. It's hard to hold onto nothing, but you aren't nothing – you're something great. Now it's time to start proving it, to yourself and to others.

Your list of accomplishments will require some thought. It will require you to think about some times and events that have not crossed your mind in years. The following is my personal list of things I've done well through the years:

In 2013, Kimberly and I hosted a family reunion, which provided a rare opportunity to have this photo taken of us with our children and grandchildren.

- Married a great wife
- Helped raise three great children
- Coached baseball, basketball, and soccer teams for all of the kids
- Won a wrestling tournament
- Still see my children
- Still talk to my children
- Still married to my first wife
- Took my wife to Hawaii four times
- Walked my daughter down the aisle
- Started a business
- Sold a business
- Taught my children to work hard
- Serve on the board of Big Brothers/Big Sisters
- Attended all of my grandchildren's birthday parties

Writing down your previous victories will help you begin to see the talents you have probably forgotten you possessed, the talents that life has beaten out of you during the past few months or years. I appreciate my friend that says to me every time he sees me, "How's life beating you?"

Your mindset has to be, "I'll do whatever I need to do to fix my personal or business problems." Tell yourself, "I can't quit this time." Repeat as needed every day, "I will work at this until God tells me to do something else."

For most men, developing a mindset of faith in God is not easy. We feel we can fix anything, do anything, and make anything work out just by sticking to it and not quitting. Well, I had to learn the hard way there is something missing when my faith is in my own abilities versus the mindset that God has a plan for me. I don't have to worry about His plan. Have a mindset of faith, even when nothing is going well.

God has told us He will work within us if we have faith as small as a mustard seed. Of course, He understands us, and I believe at times it's hard to muster any faith. He knows we would often give up if faith more than that of a mustard seed were required of us. He already knows how much faith He has put inside us. I'm thankful He didn't tell us we need to have faith the size of a watermelon! Trust in the Lord. Trust in yourself. Get to work.

Actual size of a mustard seed " . "

That's all the faith you need!

Chapter Thirty
Some Final Action Steps
and Thoughts for You to
Consider

- Make up your mind and go for it. Trust your instincts.

- Set some GOALS today. If you don't do anything else, write down some goals.

- Write the goals down with specific dates to accomplish them.

- Remember, whatever you think about will be what you move toward. So be careful what you think about.

- It doesn't matter how many times you've failed. Get up and go again.

- If you are alive, then get busy. Don't be a lazy bum.

- Your dreams are waiting on you.

- God has put every dream in you and He doesn't make mistakes.

- Believe it, and it will be yours.

  "I'll see you on the beaches where the baby blue water plays!"

"SEVEN BEHAVIORS...
...OF THE HAPPIEST AND MOST SUCCESSFUL PEOPLE ON EARTH."

If you go to a bookstore, you can find numerous books with lists of the "secrets" or "keys" for success in life. Perhaps the best-known is the late Stephen Covey's *The 7 Habits of Highly Effective People.* I have benefited personally from many of these compilations myself.

Below I'm offering to you a list of my own, what I've called "Seven Behaviors...of the happiest and most successful people on earth." It's basically a summary of principles I've learned through experience as well as interaction with successful people I've had the privilege of knowing over the years. My hope is that one or more of these will resonate with you, just another small step in your own pursuit of all God intended for you to become.

1 – The first behavior is what successful people do with their *dreams.* Successful people have dreams just like everyone else, but what they do with their dreams is where the separation occurs. It starts with a vivid picture of how the dream develops. The dream is in their mind's eye and it's there for a reason. The dream is real – so real they can see it and feel it. They can give you every specific detail of the dream, right down to the last nut and bolt. They feel the dreams are specific to them, and they are. They know they were given these dreams for a reason. And they know it's up to them to do something about them – and successful people usually do.

2 – The second behavior is out-and-out *belief* in whatever they're doing. Without belief they know it's virtually impossible to succeed in anything. Belief allows you to punch through the difficulties that inevitably will occur. Successful people know they may be the only ones in the beginning that believe an endeavor is possible. They pay little or no attention to what anyone else believes. Successful people know the first thing you have to do is believe it's possible. This, along with their commitment level, as a rule far exceeds the average person. They won't give up without a fight.

3 – The third behavior is *goal-setting*. Successful people can't live without written goals. They have goals for every area of their life. They've learned that goals have powers that are just waiting to be released. This obsession with goals comes from their knowledge and firsthand experiences with written goals. They know when you have written goals, your life can be significantly improved. They start every day knowing their goals will somehow find a way to materialize. They know things just happen for no reason at all. Successful people understand having written goals equals having a plan for their lives. It's been said that without a plan, you're planning to fail.

4 – The fourth behavior is *action*. Successful people undertake massive action if necessary to accomplish their goals. Every step they take is moving them closer to the realization of their goals. Their actions are calculated and strategic – every move has a purpose. Successful people can tell you exactly what the next step is. They strive for forward progress every day. They know there's no tomorrow. Subsequently, results must take place today – because there's *no tomorrow*.

5 – The fifth behavior is *focus*. Successful people are laser-focused. The ability to focus and concentrate takes practice. Trying to block out all of the daily distractions that are going on around us is difficult. But successful people have mastered the skill of focusing their thoughts for an extended period of time. The end results are staggering. Successful people have learned to focus their thoughts on the important matters of their lives. They're not easily distracted by small and unimportant issues. Have you ever noticed

how some people seem to spend most of their time majoring in minor things – and as a result, accomplishing very little?

6 – The sixth behavior is *passion.* Successful people are passionate about the things their involved in. Successful people are passionate about their families, their work and their hobbies. Their passion is infectious; it attracts other passionate people to the venture. Passionate people are hard to resist. Besides, who wants to hang around deadbeats? You can see it in their eyes; they have that "it" factor that can't be explained. When you're around someone with passion, you can feel their intensity.

7 – The seventh behavior of successful people is the ability to *relax.* Successful people have learned that you need to recharge your battery. Successful people have figured out to get away from the game and regroup. They know that you can't keep going and going. You have to stop and take a time-out. When they take their time-outs, they take them for both short and long periods of time. They have figured out what works for them. This keeps them looking forward to the down time and the back-in-the-game time. They work hard and they play hard; there's no in-between for them.

I've given you these Seven Behaviors for a reason. I want you to take a look at your life. How do your behaviors compare to those of successful people? No one could write down all of the behaviors that relate to success. The factors that come into play that result in success are infinite. And what works for one person is different from what works for someone else.

But here's the point I want you to grasp: As you've looked at my progressions as you read through this book, I hope you could see where, when and how I started to change my behaviors. How and when you get started is up to you. If you'll begin to form some new behaviors and habits, your life will begin to change – and change for the better.

I hope you take the lessons from this book and apply them to your life. You can go farther than anyone ever believed was possible. I believe the majority of successful people believe there is a higher power meticulously at work pointing them in the right direction and empowering them to fulfill their life's calling. When you see a breath-taking sunrise or sunset, how can you feel anything except only God could do such wondrous things?

But God won't do it all for you. And you certainly can't depend on society to do it for you. Do your part, perhaps starting with one or more of these behaviors, and God will do His part. You'll be amazed at what you can accomplish together!

By the way, you didn't skip to the last page, did you?

> Have you written your goals down?
> Write your goals down!
> Have you written your goals down?
> *Write your goals down!*

> Thank you again for reading my book.

Let me ask you one last question:
> *What are you going to do with the rest of your life?*

EDITOR'S NOTE

When Gary Highfield approached me about working with him to help in shaping and revising the manuscript for his book, I never imagined what a privilege and inspirational undertaking this would become.

Gary's not a professional writer, but the message he has presented – drawn from a lifetime of rich, often challenging, and many times unusual experiences – is one that undeniably has demanded to be said. And he's uniquely equipped to say it.

His story has been forged from hard work, determination, grit and God's grace. He gives new meaning to the phrase, "never say die." But most important, what he has to say – and the example he's become – are what many, many individuals need today.

So often, people live defeated lives, convinced they can never rise from "under the circumstances." Gary, who was born and raised in what we could consider "the wrong side of the tracks," provides compelling evidence that's not true.

Those of us that have experienced any measure of success know it cannot be achieved without initiative, imagination and inspiration. As poet T. S. Eliot wrote, "Only those who risk going too far can possibly find out how far one can go."

This is Gary's book, and I'm happy to have played a part in bringing it to reality. I sincerely hope you take to heart what he says – the illustrations from his life, his action steps, his thoughts to consider, even his poetic musings.

You're holding in your hands a treasure chest. Try to mine as many riches from it as you can.

– *Robert J. Tamasy*

About Gary Highfield

Whether you're just starting out in a career, in sales or in business, or are a seasoned veteran in the marketplace, Gary Highfield can help you.

Gary resides in Chattanooga, Tennessee, where he is a sought-after professional and corporate sales consultant and keynote speaker, dedicated to helping organizations transform their companies and their employees' lives. An entrepreneur for most of his adult life, he has helped to inspire sales teams across the country to reach their potential.

In building his own career, Gary has developed real-world strategies and training that can assist individuals and organizations in achieving their personal and corporate goals. His strategies have consistently resulted in record-breaking sales organizations.

If you're looking for sales or sales management training, mentoring, or help in finding and hiring the right people for any position, Gary's tried and true, proven and highly successful system will bring dramatic changes for you and your organization.

Passionate about making a difference, he is establishing the not-for-profit Want To Foundation, whose mission is to provide a place where people having the *"want to"* can receive help in pursuing and realizing their dreams. The foundation is in the beginning phases of development and adding board members.

A longtime bicycle enthusiast, Gary clocks more than 200 miles on his bike every week.

To contact Gary directly, you can email him at wanttobook@gmail.com, or write to him at P.O. Box 21265, Chattanooga, TN 37424.

On the Internet: To get more information about Gary and his work, to find encouragement and support through his blog, or to follow what he is currently doing, visit his website:

www.garyhighfield.com

Stay connected: You can join in conversations about Gary and his book, *When 'Want To' Becomes 'Have To!,* via social media. To get regular updates about his work, or to share him with your friends, you can find Gary on:

Facebook: FB.com/garyhighfield.author

LinkedIn: search "Gary Highfield"

Twitter: @garyhighfield7